# 90 Days to
# Success in Sales

Mark Hoxie

**Course Technology PTR**

*A part of Cengage Learning*

**COURSE TECHNOLOGY**
CENGAGE Learning™

Australia, Brazil, Japan, Korea, Mexico, Singapore, Spain, United Kingdom, United States

# COURSE TECHNOLOGY
## CENGAGE Learning™

**90 Days to Success in Sales**

**Mark Hoxie**

**Publisher and General Manager, Course Technology PTR:**
Stacy L. Hiquet

**Associate Director of Marketing:** Sarah Panella

**Manager of Editorial Services:**
Heather Talbot

**Marketing Manager:**
Mark Hughes

**Senior Acquisitions Editor:**
Mitzi Koontz

**Project Editor/Copy Editor:**
Cathleen D. Small

**Interior Layout Tech:**
Judy Littlefield

**Cover Designer:** Mike Tanamachi

**Indexer:** Valerie Haynes Perry

**Proofreader:** Kim V. Benbow

Library of Congress Control Number: 2011933250

ISBN-13: 978-1-4354-5488-0

ISBN-10: 1-4354-5488-X

**Course Technology, a part of Cengage Learning**
20 Channel Center Street
Boston, MA 02210
USA

Cengage Learning is a leading provider of customized learning solutions with office locations around the globe, including Singapore, the United Kingdom, Australia, Mexico, Brazil, and Japan. Locate your local office at: **international.cengage.com/region**.

Cengage Learning products are represented in Canada by Nelson Education, Ltd.

For your lifelong learning solutions, visit **courseptr.com**.

Visit our corporate Web site at **cengage.com**.

Printed in the United States of America

*For Abbey, Brendan, and Scott*

# Acknowledgments

First, I would like to thank my acquisitions and project editors, Mitzi Koontz at Course Technology PTR and Cathleen Small at Snyder Editorial. Little did you know, I was secretly hired to test your wits and push you to the limit as editors.... Without your patience, professionalism, and let's call them "words of inspiration," this project would have gone nowhere. The combination of your abilities and my luck to be able to work with both of you is why I am able to do what I do.

Thank you to everyone involved in making Hoxie Consulting and HoxieConsulting.com a success. Thank you to Yvette and Rose at BTI Travel for helping us launch our seminar series and Kate Thomsen for all of your support and advice. Thank you to everyone who made my first book, *90 Days to Success Marketing and Advertising Your Small Business*, a success.

Abbey, Brendan, and Scott: When my back is against the wall, you push me forward. You guys keep me going and striving for more out of my life. Matt Taranto, for 28 years you have been a friend who is always there for me through thick and thin. I could never thank you enough for everything you've done for me and the memories we've created together. Amelia, you're the smartest little girl I know—you're going to do something great with your life. Thank you to Michele for believing in me and these wild ideas that somehow come to fruition by no mistake with your love and support.

Thank you to my prior sales managers and co-workers who taught me so much about sales. This book is simply a culmination of my experiences with all of you, for better or worse. Thank you to everyone at the Onondaga County Public Library.

Mom and Dad, you've both been through so much, and I thank God every day that you had the strength to make it out on the other end. Thank you to everyone I mentioned in my last book, and to God and Trent Reznor.

# About the Author

**Mark Hoxie** began his professional career as an advertising sales representative for the yellow pages in Los Angeles. Within his first year, he was one of the top salespeople on the entire West Coast. After finding similar success in print, newspaper, radio, television, Internet, and direct-mail marketing, he returned to his hometown of Syracuse, New York, to save his family's ailing business. Using his newfound sales and marketing expertise, he brought the business back from the ashes.

Currently, Mark is working with sales teams and individual salespeople through his company, Hoxie Consulting (www.HoxieConsulting.com). He has real-world experience sitting on both sides of the table—as a sales representative and as a small-business owner. Drawing from these experiences, he has helped hundreds of salespeople improve their sales careers through workshops, seminars, and individual consultations. Mark's previous book, *90 Days to Success Marketing and Advertising Your Small Business*, helped launch the small-business marketing division of Hoxie Consulting.

# Contents

## Chapter 6: Objections . . . . . . . . . . . . . . . . . . . 67

## Chapter 9: Industry Specifics . . . . . . . . . . . . . 119

# Introduction

"He could sell ice to an Eskimo…."

Wow, what a great salesman! He can take a product that people have unlimited free access to and SELL it to them! He must be one of the best salespeople out there!

Wrong. He's a bad salesman and an even worse person. He's a conman. He's the kind of guy who perpetuates the stigma attached to salespeople. People like him are why others are reluctant to take on a sales career and consumers are defensive and uneasy when they partake in the sales process.

Selling is not about tricking people into buying something. Most people would agree with that sentiment. However, those same people might go on to push all kinds of psychological tactics, word inflection, posturing, and so on. There is certainly some validity to these theories, but they still focus more on the face-to-face sales event than on the big picture. They focus on "winning" in a battle against your potential client.

What boggles the professional mind is how countless sales authors, trainers, and theorists can spend virtually all of their time on mastering this one small portion of a sales career. Not only are they beating a dead horse, but they're also focusing on the one step in the sales process that has caused the most damage to the salesperson image.

Success in sales is based on effectively managing every aspect of your sales career.

I once signed on with a sales force that spent every minute of training on conducting meetings with potential clients. They would drill and role-play tactics, quiz us on buzzwords, have us practice (I kid you not) how to sit in a chair based on how our client was sitting in his chair, and hammer away at countless other maneuvers that had nothing to do with the product or any other facet of a sales position. Week after week, people would post bad numbers and often big, fat zeros. Training was upped, and management was dumbfounded by the lack of results.

I spent some time talking to some of the more established veterans in the office. The nice thing about a sales career is that it's easy to find people from whom to seek advice, because sales numbers are generally made public within the office. They were clearly quick-witted and had the ability to run sales meetings with ease, but they always talked about actions outside of these individual meetings that led them to success. According to them, goal setting, time blocking, a commitment to prospecting, education, and even personal life management play a major role in a successful sales career.

In time, it became evident that our sales team's problem was their inability to prospect and find new leads. Running the perfect sales meeting means nothing when you have no one to sit down in front of.

The glaring omissions found in other sales-related titles, training classes, and seminars are what led me to write this book. If you want to be successful in sales, your face-to-face sales tactics are important, but there is a laundry list of other things that go into building a prosperous sales career.

If you're looking for a shortcut to success in sales, you've picked up the right book. Flip through the pages, read some of the interesting headings, and then put the book back down on the shelf.

Now that all of the flash-in-the-pan people looking for an easy way out are gone, let's get down to business. This book doesn't give you any shortcuts or magic words that will have your buyers saying yes to all your proposals. However, this book *will* give you a well-designed roadmap to success in sales. So many other sales titles out there promise you easy results with some cliché tactics, psychological tricks, and a whole lot of motivational filler.

I drove across the country from New York to California to find my first sales job. It helped to have a map of my journey, but I didn't find any secret roads in Pennsylvania that would've put me on the West Coast in 15 minutes. Sure, an easy route would've been nice, but it's not realistic. The same can be said for sales—or any career, for that matter. *90 Days to Success in Sales* can be your roadmap to a prosperous sales career.

# Chapter 1

# Sales Basics

- My First Sales Position
- Sales Positions
- Education and Training
- Sales-Force Infrastructure
- Action Plan

Before diving into specifics about success in sales, it's important to make sure you understand some basics. Some of this may be redundant if you're a seasoned professional who has picked up this book to hone your skills. Other readers may be new to the industry and hungry for any and all information they can get their hands on. Either way, I suggest you get comfortable with this material, as it will lay the groundwork for future chapters.

## My First Sales Position

My first sales job came by way of a recruiter. She told me they had a position that might be a little over my head based on my lack of experience. But we hit it off in our initial meeting, so she figured I might do the same with her client.

"I have to warn you, this is a sales position," she said.

Warn me. Not only did I have all the preconceived notions everyone else on the outside has looking in, she had to "warn" me that selling would be involved. But I needed a better job, and my lack of education wasn't helping me land any better interviews.

I showed up for my first interview wearing a questionable pair of dress shoes that had gotten me through a few menial office jobs. The recruiter had me doubting myself from the moment my appointment was scheduled, so I was overly concerned with the small details, such as what I was wearing and how I was going to smile. When the interviewing manager stepped into the lobby, I stood up confidently to shake his hand. At that moment, one of my shoes gave out. Lucky for me, my soon-to-be-manager didn't even realize they'd given out.

After the handshake, we went into a meeting room, and I had the interview of a lifetime. What the interviewing manager never noticed was that the insole of my shoe had separated and slid to the side, exposing a bent nail that plunged deep into my foot as I stood up and stepped forward. I went home that night with a blood-soaked sock and a second interview with the district sales manager. Never flinching, I put on the façade that I was comfortable and belonged in that interview.

Little did I know, my first interview was a predictor of things to come in the world of sales. In any sales position, you'll face all kinds of adversity, objections, and rejection—far greater than that of a failing shoe. It's important to move forward no matter how difficult the hurdle or how sharp the nail.

## Job Search

Sales jobs are a dime a dozen. It's the unfortunate truth that sales positions are some of the easiest to find but the most difficult to hold onto. If you're reading this book, you probably already have a new sales position in place, but it's important to revisit the job-search process to get a clear concept of your position in the working world.

When you look online or in the newspapers, you are bound to see limitless offerings for jobs that can pay six figures for a good salesperson with little to no experience necessary. "Seeking self-motivated individuals with a desire to earn!" And yes, in most sales positions, there is the potential to make more than $100,000 a year—but the reality is that the average income is likely closer to a third or a quarter of that lofty goal.

I share this with you as a double-edged sword. You can make wheelbarrows full of money in sales, but the odds are, you will not. These positions are great because you can make so much money, but they can also be terrible because you can make so much money. Before you scratch your head about that one, let me explain.

Any job, sales or otherwise, will pay more when the difficulty and requirements are greater. More education and experience earned through hard work can lead to positions that pay a better salary. No one shows up on day one making hundreds of thousands of dollars without some kind of critical process leading up to that opportunity. In sales, you generally control a portion (if not all) of your income based on your performance.

You control at least a portion of your income based on performance.

There are two factors about the way a position pays that directly relate to the difficulty of the sale and your sales career.

Any job paying a high percentage of commission per sale is an extremely difficult sale to make. The company is investing a major portion of income to reward you for this difficult-to-close sale. Life insurance, timeshares, energy contracts, and other big-ticket and infrequent transactional sales pay this way. Think about it from a business's point of view. If you are producing a product or service that is extremely difficult to sell, you will have to offer your sales force a greater commission or potential for earning. If sales are infrequent, they must pay well to keep around career agents. If they are difficult to make, those with success must be rewarded.

On the other hand, jobs paying very low commission percentages are usually easier sales to make, but they obviously require more volume. Supply chain, materials, electronics, and other sales where the margins are smaller fall into this category.

Sales positions that pay no base salary are generally more difficult, yet they offer the highest potential for earnings. These are positions in real estate, home improvement, loans, and other areas where there is no technical limit to how many sales you can make. When sales positions offer a base salary, they tend to be a bit easier, but the overall income potential is somewhat limited. Most small-ticket retail and sales by phone operate this way.

There is nothing wrong with choosing one type of sales over another. You may like the potential to control some of your income but prefer the stability of a base salary. Or, you might want to make the most money possible, no matter what the income risk may be.

Make sure you consider a sales position that would be of interest to you. It may sound simple, but regardless of income desire, you have to believe in and/or enjoy the product or service you're peddling. You could make a lot of money in financial sales, but there's nothing wrong with selling windows if you like construction and home improvements better than financial packages. Or a potential employer might ask you to sell products that you feel are useless or that gouge consumers; remember that it's okay to have a conscience and pass on the job if you want to sleep at night.

Many sales companies employ staffing agencies and "head-hunters" to find new recruits. Make sure you get your resume to a few local employment agencies if you are looking for a sales position. Reputable recruiters can often link you up with some of the best sales opportunities in your area. Many companies will hire these agencies to do all the dirty work of weeding through the talent pool for top prospects. Based on your skills and interests, employment agencies can do a great job of helping you refine your job search.

After you've refined your job search and narrowed it down to some likely prospects, you need to think about interviewing.

## Interviewing

Unless you have an intensely honest and forthcoming sales manager, he will likely deny the following idea until his dying day: Most entry-level sales opportunities are treated the same way by management from coast to coast. They throw a bunch of salespeople against the wall and see which ones stick. If you have the ability to communicate well and present yourself professionally, you'll likely be offered the position. Of course, sales managers won't let on about the simplicity of the process. You may have two or three interviews where they ask you about your experiences, all the while feeding you information about how they've got a good feeling about you. Trust me, their "We don't hire just anyone" story will become laughable after you've spent a few months with the sales force.

Now, I can't blame sales managers entirely for this process. It's their job to motivate you to feel confident and sell their product or service. Also, the types of people who get into sales generally feed off of positive reinforcement more than most.

As easy as I've made it sound to lock up a sales position, there are some things you should remember.

First, if you've never worked in sales prior to this application, customize a version of your resume to pique a sales manager's interest. Make sure the bullet points from your previous employment focus on goals reached and other numbers-based accomplishments. You may not have worked in sales before, but showing you can hit numbers in one way or another should ensure an initial interview. If you've had sales experience, content is a little more obvious. Even if you were not successful, find some part of your experience in which you excelled.

> Customize your resume for sales positions. Focus on goals and numbers-based accomplishments.

Be on time for your interview and follow all of the other obvious protocol that goes into applying for any job. When the interviewing manager meets you, he knows that the impression he gets is the same impression you'll leave with potential clients and consumers down the road. Be presentable. Have a smile and a substantial handshake. Be confident but don't bowl them over with arrogance. As I said before, they want to make sure you are presentable and can communicate.

Expect to be questioned about your ability to handle rejection; they'll probably ask you to tell them about a time you overcame adversity. As you will learn later in this book and in your sales career, prospecting is extremely important, and you have to be prepared to hear a lot of nos. Sales managers aren't looking for people who will break down at the first sign of rejection.

During the interview process, remember that you are also interviewing the company. Make sure you get a clear picture of how they pay their sales force. Is there a base salary, and does it ever change? Will your commission percentages always be the same? If there is extended training in the beginning, do they offer training pay? The last thing you want to do is find a job you enjoy, excel, and then find out your earnings are far less than you anticipated.

As I stated earlier, landing a job as a salesperson isn't quite as difficult as the hiring company may lead on. However, you can get a good sense of their hiring standards as well as job stability by asking one simple question: "What can you tell me about the training process?"

No matter who you ask, he will tell you that they offer some of the best and most comprehensive training available for your particular field. Get the details. If you are to be off and running on day one, looking for sales, the company likely hires anyone. There might be some training materials for you to look at and a few hours here or there training, but for the most part, it's nonexistent. They want to see how quickly you can sell as soon as possible, with little risk to their bottom line. Again, this doesn't mean it's a bad position; just don't expect to be rubbing elbows with the cream of the crop. Also, you'll need to put up numbers quickly if you expect to have any longevity in a position like this.

Some companies will offer several days of full-time training in the local sales office. These guys may be a little more serious about who they hire. They're not going to want to spend a week teaching someone how to sell their product and service if they are not anticipating some level of success. They also have to extend themselves financially for a bit, especially if you have a base salary. This type of company likely won't hire just anyone for your position, but they're willing to give most professional people a shot.

The sales jobs with the most stability and the highest standards for potential candidates spend the most time and money on training. You may be flown to a training location, put up in a hotel, and paid a training allowance as well as some extra per-diem money for living away from home. If an employer is going to commit thousands—if not tens of thousands—of dollars to a new hire before they make a single sale, they're looking hard for career salespeople.

Because a sales career allows you to drive your own income level, there is far less negotiating involved with your salary than in a more traditional position. If you want to earn more, you've got to sell more. However, you may be able to secure a training allowance or even a signing bonus simply by asking.

If the training program is lackluster at best, chances are the company is willing to hire almost anyone. More intensive training programs indicate that the company is more serious about hiring a good potential candidate.

# Sales Positions

The terms discussed in this section will help you identify what type of position you currently hold and/or what type you may choose to seek out. Realistically, most sales jobs will be a combination of many types.

## Inside Sales

An inside-sales position implies that a salesperson will be doing a majority of his or her work over the phone. Inbound inside-sales positions involve the customer calling in from an advertisement or to deal with customer-service issues on an existing product or service. Outbound inside sales involves making calls to new or existing clientele to propose a product or service.

### Pros

Inside sales representatives' main tools are the phone and email. This allows them to reach far more people at a greater rate. Whereas an outside salesperson may be limited to a handful of sales meetings each day, inside salespeople can conduct dozens of sales conversations each day, depending on the product or service. Although both inside and outside salespeople conduct prospecting over the phone, inside salespeople have the advantage of turning the call into an immediate sale.

Some inside sales positions are considered to be "inbound" sales. This is when you have active buyers calling in with questions or the intention to buy. For people totally averse to prospecting, this is a position for you.

### Cons

You're a telemarketer. Depending on your product or service, your call may be considered a nuisance. Businesses expect to be solicited all day long, so their guard is up, and your access is limited. And residential consumers seem to dread sales calls even more. With the recent implementation of the federally mandated Do Not Call list, outbound sales to homes can be tedious.

If your inside position only handles inbound calls, you do not have the opportunity to prospect. Although this is a positive for some, most people know that the ability to seek out your own sales leads to the most profit potential. Also, inbound sales positions are at the mercy of their employer's marketing ability. If they can't make the phone ring, you're not going to make any sales!

Much of sales involves building rapport, and this can be very difficult to do without face-to-face meetings. Inside sales positions often focus on sales volume as opposed to sales size or quality. The high pace requirements for success in these positions can be strenuous for some people.

### Examples

Examples of inside sales positions involve credit cards, television/satellite/phone/Internet services, Internet products, transactional investing, any inbound 800-number sales, and so on.

## Outside Sales

An outside-sales position implies that a salesperson will be doing a majority of his or her work face to face with a client. The salesperson will generally have to travel locally, nationally, or even internationally to conduct business. This type of position is less governed by the clock than it is by results. If you perform well, no one is going to ask you to punch a clock. If not, expect a bit of micromanagement.

## Pros

Face-to-face meetings allow salespeople to build rapport with their clientele. The client can have a hands-on experience with a product, service, or presentation. Most outside sales positions afford people the freedom of being out of an office while also having a flexible schedule. Outside sales is one of the most profitable positions; top producers commonly earn six-figure incomes regardless of the industry.

## Cons

Longer sales processes and more time invested into each meeting make volume achievements difficult in this type of sales position. Although outside salespeople make larger and more highly commissioned sales than inside salespeople, the sales are generally more difficult to make. Outside sales requires the ability to travel and the budget for it, as outside salespeople should be prepared for periods of low or no income early on in their career.

## Examples

Examples of outside sales positions include real estate, financial services, advertising, business supply/material/services, construction, installations, pharmaceuticals and medical devices— anything that requires travel to the client.

# Retail Sales

In retail sales, customers come in to interact with the sales force. There is generally little to no prospecting. Your time is spent between an active buyer and the product you represent.

## Pros

Retail sales is generally the most stable of all sales positions, until you get into high-end products. Security and a stable income can make this a low-stress job, depending on the industry. It requires very little prospecting, which is a benefit to many people.

## Cons

A good number of retail sales positions offer little or no performance-based incentives, except for job security. You are at the mercy of the business owner's marketing and location—if no one comes in, you have no one to sell to. There is little room for income growth without a move into management or higher-end sales.

### Examples

Examples of retail sales positions include clothing, cellular phones and services, auto/boat/recreational vehicles, electronics, and furniture—anything where the customer comes to you.

## Business-to-Business Sales

Business-to-business sales positions can be retail, inside, and outside sales, but the target market is limited to other businesses.

### Pros

Most companies have exponentially higher budgets than individuals, and they usually expect to be doing business with you or your competition. Unlike consumer sales, you work with a business budget as opposed to a limited personal budget. Further, business owners expect to be solicited from all angles, so there is less stress about feeling invasive.

These kinds of sales careers can yield very high income, depending on the product or service. And, business-to-business sales can be conducted during business hours, as opposed to consumer sales, which have to cater to nights and weekends.

### Cons

Because of the high-value benefits to this sales type, competition is extremely stiff in virtually all industries. And, with larger budgets to be spent, more people are soliciting businesses, so your opportunities may be limited. These entrepreneurs have heard it all and often give you very little time to work with. Also, business owners have gatekeepers who are trained to keep you away if they so choose.

### Examples

Examples of business-to-business sales positions include advertising, pharmaceuticals, supply chain, staffing agencies, and distributors—any position that requires dealing with businesses of all sizes.

## Business-to-Consumer Sales

In a consumer sales position, you will be selling to individuals, generally to meet their personal needs and wants.

## Pros

Compared to the number of businesses out there, consumer salespeople have a virtually limitless sea of potential customers. Consumers tend to be an "easier" sell. Unlike business owners, they are solicited a fraction of the time. They can make purchases based on emotion and are not as concerned with details as business owners tend to be.

## Cons

Consumers generally have smaller budgets than business clientele. Also, the sales process can feel more invasive, as it's uncomfortable for some consumers. Further, the federally backed Do Not Call list can make it difficult to sort through leads and can even result in stiff fines and penalties for the company you represent.

## Examples

Examples of business-to-consumer sales positions include home improvements, automobiles, credit cards, and most retail—any position where your client is an individual consumer.

# Inbound Sales

Inbound sales describes any sales position where your clients come to you without your personal solicitation. The company you work for may advertise and market to customers, but they initiate contact with you.

## Pros

There's no prospecting—if your company advertises well and has a good product or service, people will be lining up to buy. The sales process becomes thinned almost to an order-taking position, making it an easier career choice for people uncertain about selling. You have an active buyer in front of you, generally expecting to deal with a salesperson.

## Cons

These positions do not generally pay as much as other sales opportunities, as consumers are already in front of you and ready to make a buying decision. Many of these positions are associated with inside sales and rely on high volumes of activity. As stated earlier, your activity is driven by your company's ability to market and make their own phones ring. You don't have the opportunity to go out and bring in more business of your own.

### Examples

Examples of inbound sales positions include retail, automobiles, 800 numbers, service and website call centers—any position where the customer comes to you.

## Outbound Sales

Outbound sales positions are the most traditional form of sales. Your job duties rely heavily on prospecting and soliciting new clientele.

### Pros

What you do with your opportunity is up to you. Unless you are working in protected territories, you can solicit anyone you feel could benefit from your product or service. These are generally the highest-paying sales jobs, as you must go and seek out your own clientele.

### Cons

What you do with your opportunity is up to you. If you're not self-motivated and you have a problem with prospecting and rejection, you're not going to make much money or last very long. Some managers will push you to sell to your "circle of influence," such as friends and family members. Although outbound sales-people do get some forms of inbound business from time to time, it's never enough to grow on.

### Examples

Examples of outbound sales positions include financial services, real estate, advertising, business services, self-employment—any career where you're chasing down potential clients rather than them chasing down you.

In the last chapter of this book, we will discuss and dissect popular sales fields in a similar fashion, along with discussing industry specifics.

# Education and Training

The best salespeople know their product inside out and have an honest interest in what they sell. You have to be passionate about your product and ready to explain any and all features and benefits it may offer.

Companies will offer you a wide range of training opportunities. Most will help you start your career with an initial training process or, at worst, some materials for self-study.

Early on, you'll be eager to hit the ground running. It might seem as if nothing could be better than finishing up training and getting in front of your clients. I cannot stress enough how important it is for you to take full advantage of every bit of training you can get your hands on. Be present and attentive for all training classes. Take advantage of all training materials and product information your company shares with you.

Take advantage of all training opportunities offered by your employer.

If you start your position with a fully immersed training program, make it your job to absorb every bit of every lesson possible.

When I was in training for my first job in advertising sales, we were scheduled to have a test after the first week of training. They educated us on every single in and out of yellow-pages advertising. We were provided with codes for every ad type, crucial content for ad design, contract and layout requirements—anything you would ever need to know about the yellow pages as a whole. I paid attention in class, studied at night, and had no problems with the exam on Friday.

For some reason, it never occurred to me that there was going to be a score to determine who passed and who failed, though I do remember them saying that people who failed would have to take the test again on Monday. My point here isn't to brag about classroom accomplishments, because it was actually my ignorance and lack of experience that helped me find success. Because I had never been formally trained or tested for a job, I assumed you had to know it all. I aced the test along with one other salesperson. The majority of my classmates scored in the 70s—just high enough to proceed to the next part of training. In hindsight, it's no surprise that most of the class fizzled out of sales within the first six months, while the other teacher's pet and I had several years of great success. There may have been other things that kept us at the top of the heap, but knowing my product inside and out was crucial.

After you've worked through the classes and materials you've been exposed to, seek out continued education on your own. I'm not talking about dropping money at the local community college; I'm suggesting you research your industry outside of what you've been provided with. If you get to know about your competition, consumer views of your product, its history, and training tips from other professionals, you can only set yourself up for even more success. Use the Internet to visit competitors' websites—simply type the name of your product or service into a search engine and see what comes up!

Outside of the training you are provided, your company may have marketing materials that you can send out or use in your meetings with potential clients. Be sure you learn those inside out as well. They contain pertinent information, and you should be extremely comfortable with them if you want to incorporate them into your sales meetings.

# Sales-Force Infrastructure

The last thing that you want slowing down your success in sales is a snafu in the office. It is important to understand the flow of your sale after your client signs off on a purchase. In some positions, your client will walk off with the product, but in others, the signature is just the start of a long process. Understanding the lay of the land and office politics will help you avoid any unforeseen roadblocks to your success.

## Support Staff

Follow the Golden Rule: Treat support staff and co-workers well, and they will likely do the same to you.

Treat the office support staff better than your own family! Many people likely will be involved at some point in your sales process. People working as receptionists, assistants, underwriters, clerks, and so on are all there to streamline the sales process. It's simple respect and logic: Treat them well, and they will treat you well.

If you're missing a signature, but you've been complaining to the underwriter about her speed and never so much as given a glance in her direction, expect her to give you the bare-minimum effort in return. If you've been a decent and appreciative person, she likely will get in touch with you as soon as possible and may even leave you with a blank form so you can get right back to your client to fix the error.

Buy the receptionist lunch once in a while! Do you want someone to play favorites when new clients call the main line? Do you want someone to tell you the moment a fax comes across the machine? A simple lunch might go a long way....

In my experience, people who treat the support staff with kindness and appreciation have the fewest logistical problems with the sales process. Those who complain, badmouth, and look down upon these hourly workers somehow seem to perpetuate their own unhappiness with the post-sale flow.

## Management

It's important to remember that your managers are there to support you. They're not selling, yet they're typically paid based on your performance. They do well when you do well. If you have a manager who micromanages, and it's throwing off your sales process, have a conversation. If your manager is too hands off, ask for help.

Too often, people in the sales world have a sense of "me versus my manager." This attitude can lead to missed opportunities for both parties. Establish an open line of communication with your manager and be completely forthcoming. If you hide things and constantly run into surprises, it will stress your relationship. Your manager won't trust you, and you'll feel hassled by her.

Be open and communicative with your sales manager. He's working *with* you, not *against* you.

Almost about every conversation you have with your manager will be about sales numbers. If you take one thing away from this chapter, remember this: Under-promise and over-deliver. You may have heard this sentiment in one form or another, but it couldn't be any more pertinent than when it comes to your relationship with management. Any time you come up short, you will be questioned, doubted, and kept under a more watchful eye. If you're always under-projecting your sales numbers, your manager will almost never have a way to give you grief.

This leads me to one more secret that managers would prefer to take to the grave: Asking you to project sales numbers has nothing to do with them forecasting a sales period. They always want an "accurate" number that they can report to their bosses—so "accurate" that they frequently pressure you into projecting a higher number. Once you've projected a higher number, guilt becomes an additional motivating factor. Don't let them sway you—under-promise and over-deliver.

## Salespeople

One of the craziest paradoxes in all of sales is that you're working side by side with people who are your direct competition. Unless you have a protected sales territory, anything goes. That being said, treating one another with respect and honesty will make your life in the office or storefront far less stressful. If you operate with a cutthroat attitude, expect the same in return.

Salespeople are inherently competitive. This can make for some lighthearted office competition, but it's important not to step on any toes. Yes, you could make a few extra bucks from time to time by calling on a co-worker's lead, but for the longevity of your career, it's important to build good relationships with the rest of your sales team. There may be a time when you need their help. There may be a time when they are motivated to operate honestly with you because you have been decent with them. If one of your leads is accidentally directed to your office nemesis, do you really think you'll ever get that lead back?

# Action Plan

If you're not employed in sales:

✓ Identify the type of sales job you would be most comfortable in. (Remember to consider the type of sales process and how you will be compensated.)

✓ Apply with employment or staffing agencies.

✓ Customize a resume for sales jobs to which you are applying.

✓ Think about success stories you can share during your interview.

✓ Present yourself as a positive professional, inside and out.

If you're employed in sales:

✓ Define your position's sales process and compensation.

✓ Consider training that is available to you for areas that you have not yet mastered.

✓ Research your industry, competitors, marketing materials, and so on.

✓ Make positive acquaintances with everyone in your office.

# Chapter 2

# Initial Prospecting

- Cold Leads versus Warm Leads
- Targeting Your Leads
- Prospecting Types
- Language and Content
- Case Studies
- Personal Marketing
- Prospecting Theory
- Action Plan

Prospecting is the first and the single most important step to the sales process. If you have no one to sell to, there is no sale. The more people you have to sell to, the more money everyone makes. You may know your product inside out, but that won't amount to a single dime unless you have someone sitting across the table from you. You could have the best communication and people skills, but nothing gets sold until there is a buyer.

Prospecting refers to the act of seeking out new customers and clients.

Prospecting is the act of seeking out new customers and clientele. Depending on your industry, a good portion of sales may be to existing accounts, but even those were prospected for at the relationship's inception. As important as it is to nurture existing relationships, bringing new ones to the table is exponentially more profitable to your company and your own pocket.

The process of prospecting is the number-one reason why people do not go into sales. It's also unquestionably the least appealing step in the sales process for active salespeople. No one wants to hear the word no. Worse yet, no one wants to hear, "Leave me alone; you salespeople are all vultures!"

Prospecting takes people out of their comfort zone. So much of sales is about building relationships, yet this initial contact can often be awkward and unfriendly. This is why prospecting is often referred to as "cold calling."

The key to effective prospecting is "warming" your well-targeted leads.

## Cold Leads versus Warm Leads

Any potential client with whom you've never had contact and you have no established connections is considered a cold lead. You may be working out of a yellow pages or a list provided by your employer or another source.

Cold leads are those you've never had contact with; warm leads are those you already have a connection with.

Warm leads include anyone who you may already have a connection with. You might have called on them previously, established a relationship based outside of sales, or even sourced them through a referral. What makes these leads so valuable is that you have an "in" and a way to break the ice when making contact.

# Targeting Your Leads

Just as a business must develop a marketing strategy to find success, as a sales rep you must have a plan of attack. Businesses and salespeople alike must define their primary demographics to have a better rate of return. If you're selling uniform services to businesses, for example, it's probably not worth your time to call a law firm where everyone wears normal personal attire. A homeowner's insurance salesperson is probably not going to want to call on people living in retirement apartments. Although these examples are rather obvious, they make a good point: It's important for you to refine your target audience before you set out to solicit.

Defining your target demographic will give you a better rate of return on sales.

# Prospecting Types

There are many ways you can prospect, and you can use numerous strategies to make sure your approach is warm and directed at the right people. Certain sales jobs may have limitations based on the parameters of the position. Regardless, though, you will be able to draw from theories behind one avenue or use them in combination, as you will see in the case studies after this section.

## Phoning

The telephone is the number-one tool in the world of prospecting. You can reach out to hundreds of potential clients in a very short amount of time. However, rejection levels may be high because you're seen initially as a telemarketer. And it might seem as if handling rejection over the phone would be easier than doing so face to face, but in reality, the people you are soliciting can get quite bold over the phone.

### Pros

If you have enough leads to work with, you can make hundreds of calls in a short amount of time. Whether you plan to meet face to face or talk again over the phone, the call becomes easier when you're seeking out an appointment as opposed to an immediate sale.

### Cons

Clicks and dial tones. As easy as it is for you to pick up the phone and place a call, it's twice as easy for your potential client to hang up. Also, it is required by law that you check the number with the national Do Not Call registry to avoid penalties for you and your company.

### What Works

If you have the time and budget, consider warming your cold leads with a letter or an email. This gives you an opportunity to call about that letter you sent last week—which can be easier than making a straight cold call. Unless your job requires you to do so, avoid getting into a sales discussion over the phone. Your goal should always be to set up an appointment at a later date for a formal phone or face-to-face meeting.

## Face to Face

Although phoning is the most traditional form of initial contact, some people are more comfortable prospecting on foot.

### Pros

Face-to-face interaction with your leads can give you a better opportunity to establish rapport and schedule a meeting. It's more difficult to say no to someone's face than it is to do so over the phone—let alone be rude about it.

Face-to-face prospecting can be just as intrusive to your prospect's day, but that can often work to your advantage. Prospects may hang up on you if you call, but when you're standing in front of your lead, you may be more likely to score a future appointment simply so they can get on with their day. If you have any leave-behinds or marketing materials, this is also a good way to get prospects prepped before a formal meeting.

### Cons

It can be a very time-consuming process to walk into a business or go door to door to set an appointment or make a sale. Depending on who you're visiting, it may be quite intrusive for you to walk into their business or show up on their front step. Some businesses will post "No Solicitation" signs, so it may be a better idea to seek out a different route in that case. Your manager may tell you differently, but I've never had someone who has posted a "No Solicitation" sign be overly happy at my unannounced appearance.

### What Works

Map out your plan of attack. I've known a lot of salespeople who prospect aimlessly on foot (that is, by car) that simply eat up time. Also, make your unannounced appearances relatively unarmed. If you show up at someone's door with a huge pull-behind brief-case and papers everywhere, your prospect will have his guard up immediately. Consider coming in with just a notebook or one piece of leave-behind literature. That being said, make sure you do have more material handy if possible, just in case you catch your prospect at a good time.

## Mail/Email

Mail and email are also effective ways to reach out to clients, and many salespeople never consider these tactics.

### Pros

Reaching out through mail or email is a very low-pressure approach. Your lead will likely give you a paragraph or two of consideration without putting up his guard against a live salesperson. Mail is generally used as a way to warm leads, as you will have to follow up with a call or visit to make this method effective. This soft touch will also give your prospect a chance to think about or research your product or service and be mentally prepared for your initial solicitation.

### Cons

Postage can add up, and unless you have a decent personal budget or allowance from your employer, it might be cost prohibitive. You can send emails without cost, but they have a worse response rate than direct mail, and scraping together email addresses can be exceedingly time consuming.

Further, the soft advantage of this approach can also be a disadvantage. Many leads will disregard your message altogether. And don't expect them to pick up the phone to make the first contact, or you'll be waiting for quite some time.

### What Works

If it is financially possible, use this tool as a means of warming up your leads. Let them know in less than one paragraph why doing business with you will be advantageous to them. Then give them a timeframe in which they can expect your call. Email in the same manner, but don't waste your time unless you have a qualified list or some individuals in whom you've already invested time.

## Events

Networking and other social events can be a great way to meet new prospects and provide a brief introduction to you and your service.

### Pros

In a social setting, most people will have their guard down to people prospecting for sales. They're expecting to meet and mingle with others, so it won't be intrusive when you tell them about what you do (assuming you keep your spiel to less than a minute). You might be able to secure an in-person meeting with someone if you immediately pique his or her interest, but ultimately you're giving yourself an in for when you call on that prospect in the near future.

### Cons

Depending on your line of business, it might be difficult to find the right kinds of prospects grouped together at once. And these events can be costly if there is a cover charge and fees for drinks, food, and so on. Also, you might find that the timing will cut into your evenings, weekends, and other times intended for family and personal use. When the title "networking event" is thrown around, you can expect it to be a bunch of other salespeople shuffling business cards.

### What Works

I'm not saying you should steer clear entirely of networking events—you can sell to other salespeople, so they're not a total loss—but I would not let them consume the bulk of your free time. Consider other social events where people are not expecting to be prospected as leads: community meetings, sporting events, fundraisers—anywhere you have the opportunity to strike up a conversation with a complete stranger. While at an event, be sociable and ask your potential lead about what he does for a living. Get him to open up a bit, and he will reciprocate, providing you with an in to give him a quick explanation of what you do.

Don't be afraid to offer up a business card, as this will encourage the lead to do the same. If he doesn't have a card, make sure you take note of his full name so you can research at a later date. Just make sure you write it down after your conversation is through, or you'll be sure to forget it.

# Language and Content

No matter what approach you use, make sure you have a hook—a reason for your prospect to accept a time-sensitive appointment or to allow you to continue with your call. Here are some examples of hooks to be used after introduction with cold leads, both face to face and over the phone:

> "I am calling you today because our rates are up for review at the end of the month, and I'd like a chance to sit down with you before that happens."

> "I've worked with many other [businesses/families/doctors] in the past, but I know we haven't had a chance to get together yet."

> "Our company is running a special on [windows/memberships/ Internet service] this month, and I want to make sure you have a chance to take advantage of these offers."

Make it clear (without going into the sales process) that there could be a potential benefit to your meeting. Taking advantage of warm leads gives you an even easier hook and allows for some more comfortable verbiage:

> "I have been working with Bob Smith for a while now, and he suggested I give you a call."

> "I'm calling in regard to a letter I sent last week. I'm hoping you've had a chance to review it so we can set up a meeting later next week."

> "We met at the chamber mixer last month, and I thought I would give you a call."

Whatever your hook may be, the language can play a big role in whether you get the appointment or sale. Some sale professionals like the assumptive close for setting a meeting:

> "…and that's how we can help you. So, do you want to meet Wednesday at 1 p.m. or at 4?"

This tactic can work well if you've still hooked the client, but just as with any other message, it shouldn't sound canned. I can't tell you how many times I've been on the phone with a salesperson who reads off a three-minute script, finishes with two appointment times, and then comes up for air. Make it sound natural and don't be afraid to get some confirmation from your lead throughout your *quick* appointment-setting process.

# Case Studies

Here are some examples of how people in various sales positions can prospect. Although these are industry specific, you can draw from any of these examples.

## Case Study 1

Martha Mason, home security

Martha realizes that new homeowners are some of the top prospects for home security systems. She pays a small fee to have access to her county's new home sales transactions. Once per month, she sends out a welcome letter with a brief introduction to her company's services. About two weeks after the mailing, she calls new homeowners, echoing and expanding on the content of her letter.

Martha was able to make a small investment to help reach out to qualified leads. The well-timed welcome letter warmed up the homeowners and gave her a reason to call for an appointment.

## Case Study 2

Tim Jefferson, web development

Tim collects advertisements containing local websites. He holds onto newspapers, magazines, and direct mail and jots down sites he sees on television or hears on the radio. After visiting each of these sites, he saves the email contacts he comes across in a spreadsheet. Tim emails each of these potential leads, congratulating them for marketing their site well and offering up his company's services to help them get the most out of their marketing efforts. He closes each email by stating his intent to call in the near future.

Tim prequalified his leads by finding companies invested in marketing their websites. By reaching out to the ones that obviously needed some attention (without being negative), he avoids wasting his time collecting email addresses of uninvolved businesses. He now has a reason to call his prospects to ask for a first appointment.

## Case Study 3

Jeff Meany, life insurance

Jeff commits to seeking out leads through social events. The local chamber has a sizable networking event each month that he attends. He also joins his high school's alumni association and becomes a regular at all of their gatherings. A baseball enthusiast, Jeff becomes a Little League coach. As Jeff gets to know people through these groups and events, he becomes recognizable as a nice guy but also as an insurance sales professional. As he builds warm relationships through these associations, he casually asks people whether they've reviewed their life-insurance needs recently.

Because Jeff built up relationships with people on a personal level and made numerous contacts from his exposure, he had the opportunity to have comfortable opening conversations with many people. Although this tactic takes time, the long-term results are worth the time investment. Of course, Jeff would need to supplement this process with other sales early on, but this is an excellent way to make a career out of a sales position.

## Case Study 4

Ellen Waters, employment agency

Ellen works for a large national employment agency. Although her position allows her to solicit any company in the United States, she refines her sales process by paying attention to growth trends. She cross-references regions with population spurts against industry growth before she calls on companies with the highest likelihood for employment needs. When she makes her calls, she can expect to have a better conversion rate.

Although Ellen had no real ability to warm her leads (because she works on a national level), by highly targeting whom she calls, she can have a better expected rate of sales. She also has an immediate opening where she can talk about the growth she studied to find her leads in the first place.

## Personal Marketing

Being a salesperson can be very similar to running your own business. For one thing, your profits are based on your performance. Some pure-commission sales positions are quite literally your own small business if you're paid on a 1099, like a contractor.

*Can you market yourself to bring in new business, like real-estate agents do?*

With these similarities, it's possible to draw some strategy in sales from the entrepreneurial world. Companies need to advertise and market themselves, and with some sales positions, this is a great way to bring in new business. Real estate is one of the few sales industries where agents have taken on the process of self-branding and advertising. But what about other industries? What's to say a home-energy salesperson couldn't put a little ad in the church bulletin? What's stopping a beverage-route salesman from putting a small ad in a local business journal? Just be sure to check with your management before you run any kind of ads—you need to make sure you're not stepping on anyone's toes. Chances are they'll be thrilled by your initiative.

## Prospecting Theory

If you look around any sales company, you will find that the top sales reps aren't afraid to prospect. They may be at the point in their career where they only have to maintain accounts or sell to an established group of people or businesses, but rest assured they started their careers prospecting. If you have your doubts, watch the way these seasoned reps go after the occasional lead that comes across their desk. They're fearless—calling anyone without hesitation and often not worrying about whether the lead is even warm.

*To make a career out of sales, you have to make a career out of prospecting.*

If you want to make a career out of sales, you must make a career out of prospecting. It's important that you practice any scripts your company provides so that they become second nature and don't sound scripted. Many sales companies throw new blood into the prospecting world with scripts and let them pick up the phone and read away. As long as they're making hundreds of calls or walking in on dozens of businesses daily, companies know the reps will get some sales by default. But you can do better. Take the scripts you're given, make them your own, and learn to use them in a way that's natural to you.

Although prospecting may wear you down over time, it's important that you never let your prospecting fatigue show when you're calling on potential clients. If you're making your 380th call of the day and it's apparent, you're already starting off on the wrong foot before you even pick up the phone. If you're tired out and racing through a memorized script, you're going to alienate the person on the other end of the line. Take time to reset your mind before each call; it will help you find more success later in the calling day. If you're legitimately worn out, take a break. Just like any other physical or mental activity, prospecting can be difficult to do for an extended period of time. That being said, don't let that become an excuse for why you're not prospecting.

> Take a break when you need it. If you sound tired on your prospecting calls, you'll leave the potential client with a negative first impression.

It's important that you consider the benefit of your service to your potential client before you call. No one wants to hear another salesperson calling to tell him how great a product or service is. Uncover a real need your clients typically have and share that with your lead. Some sales reps may be tempted (or even trained) to say something like this:

"Our payroll service is the best in town. We'll beat anyone's prices, and we have convenient online payroll entry."

Most business owners are far more concerned with their day than with how great your company is. Listen to how this approach addresses the lead's needs right off the bat:

"I know many business owners are concerned with the cost of a payroll service, and that's where we can help."

Immediately, the prospect's thought is, "Yes, payroll is expensive, and I've been thinking about making some cuts." If you've caught the person at the right time and presented yourself in a pleasant and professional fashion, he may agree to hear you out.

It is also important to be ready to prospect at any given time. You will find that social events and random conversations sparked anywhere can lead to a potential client. As a salesperson, you should have your own "commercial" for getting people interested in the product or service you offer. Make sure you have something you're comfortable with and that is more complex than simply saying, "I sell mortgages."

For example:

> **Prospect:** So what do you do?
>
> **Salesperson:** Well, you know how the government has tightened restrictions on home loans? I help homebuyers make sure they meet the new qualifications, and then I match them up with the right kind of loan.

In this example, the salesperson displayed a universal need, showed how he can "help" as opposed to sell, and described the solution process. In just two short sentences, he gave a lot more life to his position than simply saying, "I sell mortgages." Now, the person he is talking to may start asking questions or show some curiosity because of his unique commercial.

Depending on the length of your sales process, it's important to determine whether your goal for calling is to set an appointment for a sales consultation or to sell as soon as you reach your lead. It can be quite different between industries, and that will usually dictate the direction of the call. Generally speaking, it's best to set an appointment and spend the least amount of time possible talking about the features and benefits of your product. If you start having conversations like that, they will end abruptly with, "How much is this going to cost?" Other sales professionals will tell you that is a buying signal, but in reality it's simply a signal that the end of your conversation is imminent. If you rush the sales process over the phone or within a few minutes of meeting, you'll have no rapport with your potential customer, and the likelihood of you earning a sale will go way down.

Attitude is important throughout the entire sales process, including your time spent prospecting. This is not a complex theory: People want to do business with calm and pleasant people. Business owners' and consumers' lives are stressful enough; they don't need to add another negative experience into the mix. If you come across as a downer, people aren't going to give you the time of day. To the other extreme, if you're pushy and over-the-top excited about everything in the world, people will sense that you're just another pushy salesman.

It's easy to burn out in a sales career if you get emotionally tied to the prospecting process. Even the best salespeople get shut down by prospects on a daily basis. You must get used to hearing no more often than yes. With smart prospecting, you can refine the process, but you'll never be able to eliminate rejection.

# Action Plan

✓ Determine your target demographic for solicitation.

✓ Decide what scripts and education you can use to become more comfortable with cold calling.

✓ Determine what methods you will use to prospect for new leads.

✓ Develop a hook for setting an appointment or making a sale.

✓ Prepare a personal "commercial" so that when you have a chance to tell someone what you do, you can be concise while still drawing people in.

✓ Draft a few versions of a letter you can use to warm your leads.

✓ Consider what types of advertising might help you bring in new leads.

# Chapter 3

# Initial Sales Meeting

- Building Rapport
- Case Studies
- Line of Questioning
- Uncovering Client Needs
- Action Plan

No matter how long the sales process takes in your particular industry, there is always an initial meeting with your potential client. This usually entails a bit of rapport-building, discovery, and fact-finding. Your goal is to build an amiable connection with your client and determine whether there is potential for a mutually beneficial relationship. In a typical sales process, this is often an entire formal meeting. Other industries that have a shorter sales process, such as retail or telemarketing, may cover these areas in just the first few minutes of a conversation.

## Building Rapport

Finding salespeople who can build rapport is where many hiring managers miss the mark. It's commonly thought that the most outgoing, well-spoken person with "people skills" makes for the best kind of salesman. In reality, this kind of personality can alienate a good portion of the population.

Think back to high school. Think about the most outgoing and popular person you remember—the guy or gal who would light up any room he or she walked into. Now remember the quiet kid with straight A's. Both of these people were likely destined for some level of success. However, how well do you think they would hit it off when it comes to building a personal or professional relationship?

*Great communications and people skills aren't the keys to building rapport—acting is.*

The key to building rapport isn't great people skills or robust communication, it's acting. Now, "acting" might not seem like the most honest approach, but tailoring your persona to your potential client will make him feel comfortable much more quickly. Some sales gurus adhere to this concept and even go as far as to suggest that you match your posture and facial expressions to that of your client. But unless you've recently won an Academy Award, you're probably going to humiliate yourself if you take it that far.

Introduce yourself in the most calm and nondescript fashion possible. Pretty quickly, you should be able to get a sense of your client's demeanor. Use your common sense and present yourself in a way that you feel makes the most sense. If a person is shy, don't bowl her over with personality. It might feel uncomfortable, but if you come across as timid too, you won't push a shy person out of her comfort zone. Conversely, if another client comes across as confident and aggressive, don't use that same timid personality, or the more assertive client may not take you seriously.

Regardless of the persona you put forward, there is one thing you need to remember nine times out of ten when building rapport: Less is more. People want to talk about themselves. They feel better and make more positive decisions when they get to do the talking. Even the shy ones will boast about their needs, wants, and accomplishments when properly asked.

When it comes to building rapport, less is more.

Typical consumers spend their time working for a living. They answer to their bosses, spouses, children, and family, so any outlet they can find is a welcome one. Business owners respond well to the same opportunity to speak, but for different reasons. Most successful business owners take a lot of pride in what they do. Their confidence in their product or service is likely what led them to the position they are in. Let them brag about their business and tell you about their accomplishments. Ask them leading questions that will allow them to open up.

I can't tell you the number of times I've sat across from a client for half an hour, listening to them talk, only to have them finish with, "You know, you're a really nice guy!" Was it the cumulative 90 seconds of talking I'd done in the half hour? I'm a pretty confident person, but I don't think it had anything to do with the pinch of small talk and leading questions. When people open up and talk, they feel good about themselves and, therefore, good about their experience with you.

When you're trying to build rapport, adapt to your surroundings. This is most applicable when you are meeting with business owners at their location or consumers at their home or work. You'll find some of the best icebreakers or openers simply by looking around the room. If you see a bunch of mounted fish, ask about where they were caught. If there are decades-old pictures from when the business was founded, ask about its history. Take clues from your surroundings to touch upon the things most interesting to your potential client.

Look around your environment to find icebreakers and conversation starters.

You should also read the newspaper. Or if not, at least pull up their website each morning for the top local news. This is one of the best outside tools at your disposal for building rapport.

This tactic is especially important if you're working with business owners. You never know where your opening conversation may go. There may be talk of changing the county sales tax, which will affect their business. Your conversation starter could also be something as far out as a bug spraying scheduled for the business's neighborhood. Or maybe the owner's favorite local sports team won the night before. Staying on top of local news, politics, and sports can help you relate better to your clientele. Better yet, staying on top of local issues and advertisements may lead you to some new leads to call on!

# Case Studies

Here are some great examples of how to open up an initial sales meeting. Note the way each salesperson creates a bit of rapport and reacts to what the customers present them with.

## Case Study 1

Name: Mary

Industry: Medical-device sales

Client: Dr. Gibbons

Business/consumer: Podiatrist

Mary has scheduled a first meeting with Dr. Gibbons. Upon arriving at his office, she notices that in the waiting area, most of the magazines are sailing and nautical themed. When she's called in to meet with the doctor, she notices several pictures of Dr. Gibbons and his family on boats and in tropical locations. Their conversation begins thusly:

**Mary:** Thanks for taking the time to meet with me today, Dr. Gibbons.

**Dr. Gibbons:** No problem, Mary. I usually meet with reps on my lunch break.

**Mary:** I notice you've got all kinds of sailing pictures here in your office.

**Dr. Gibbons:** Yeah, when my family and I manage to get away, we do a lot of sailing around the Florida Keys.

**Mary:** That's great! My uncle kept a boat in Newport, Rhode Island, and I used to love heading out to visit during the summer.

**Dr. Gibbons:** You know, I haven't spent as much time sailing up north in the cooler waters. My wife prefers getting away to the warmer weather.

**Mary:** Oh, she's into sailing, too? Are you teaching your children to sail as well?

Mary took the obvious route of talking with Dr. Gibbons about sailing, based on what she saw in the office. He's on his lunch break and likely glad to keep it casual. Notice that so far in the conversation, Mary has not redirected the discussion to her point of business. Instead, she made a personal connection to his passion by mentioning her uncle and took a genuine interest in his hobby.

If you have a lengthy sales process, feel free to let this initial sales meeting go off on any course your client sees fit. Let the client redirect you to the sales process when he realizes that he has been doing all the talking and the topic has solely been his own interests. It's time well spent at putting new customers at ease in your presence.

## Case Study 2

Name: Tom

Industry: Television advertising

Client: Christopher

Business/consumer: Bar and grill

On the way to his first meeting with Christopher, Tom notices some bulldozers clearing out a lot close to his destination. He recalls reading an article about a highly contested hotel getting the go-ahead to start building just two blocks away from Christopher's Bar & Grill. Tom and Christopher's conversation begins thusly:

**Tom:** Thank you for taking the time to meet with me today, Christopher!

**Christopher:** You're welcome. We've been looking to grow our business a bit, so we thought it was a good time to look into further advertising.

**Tom:** That's great! Speaking of growth, I heard about that new hotel coming in right around the corner.

**Christopher:** Yeah, we're excited about it. We do get a little bit of the business-traveler crowd, but this should do great things for us.

**Tom:** I would imagine so. Hopefully, you can establish a good relationship with them so they send out-of-town guests your way.

Tom is on top of the local news, so he was able to recall a pertinent piece of information related to his client's business. Notice how Tom mentioned the hotel in a very open-ended manner. There's always a chance that Christopher would *not* be into the expansion, so Tom tested the waters first by simply stating what he'd heard. Christopher might have been upset and could have stated that along with the hotel, there would be a competing restaurant in the building—a fact that would have strengthened his need for Tom's advertising solutions but also given Tom the cue not to be excited about the new development.

## Case Study 3

Name: Scott

Industry: Window installations

Client: Mrs. Peters

Business/consumer: Homeowner

Scott has a sales-and-estimate appointment for new windows scheduled at the home of Mrs. Peters. Immediately upon his arrival, Mrs. Peters has her arms folded tightly and does not invite Scott in. She's clearly reserved and protective of her personal space, so Scott doesn't force her to open up or even offer to shake her hand.

**Scott:** Good morning, Mrs. Peters. I'm here to give you an estimate for your new windows.

**Mrs. Peters:** Yes, we'd like a quote on all windows being replaced except for the basement and attic windows.

**Scott:** Well, I'll just need to walk around and take some measurements. Would you like to walk with me so you can point out anything I need to be aware of?

**Mrs. Peters:** Sure.

The two walk around the house as the measuring begins. Scott notices a well-kept garden close to the back of the house.

**Scott:** Our guys will make sure to protect your landscaping back here.

**Mrs. Peters:** Good. When we had our house painted, a lot of this got trampled.

**Scott:** That's too bad, but it really looks great now.

Right away, Scott realized that his potential client was not interested in small talk or typical rapport-building steps. Even still, he invited her along for the slight chance that he would be able to build rapport. Noticing the nice garden, he made a non-personal comment by relating it to his business, knowing it was something she likely took pride in. His lack of pushiness and respect for her personal space will likely lead to a sale if the price is within range.

A few other less traditional ideas can help you in the rapport-building process. With today's technology, it's easy to learn quite a bit about any industry—or any person for that matter. If you have time to plan before meeting your client, throw the person's name into a search engine. Maybe you'll find out that she is on the board of directors for a local animal hospital. Maybe he is the proud parent of a local high-school athlete. The more you know about your customer, the better. If you come up with something far out and unusual, just come at them with pure honesty.

> "I was doing a little research before our meeting, Joyce, and I discovered that you're an accomplished sculptor!"

Obviously, you should pick and choose the tidbits you bring to the table.

> "I was doing a little research before our meeting, Joyce, and I saw that you've got a $150,000 tax lien on your home!"

Probably not the best one to use unless you work for a tax-relief company....

Your research should also include brushing up on whatever industry your client is involved in. Maybe you've never sat down with an estate attorney, or you have no idea what a phytologist does. (It's someone who writes about plants, in case you were wondering.) Becoming a little more comfortable with your clients' background can only help. It might help you to become better suited to navigate their needs, or maybe you'll find out about some breaking news in their industry or a change they may be dealing with in the near future.

## Line of Questioning

Rapport lays the foundation for any functional relationship, but eventually it's time to move on to business. Once the ice is broken and the relationship is warmed up, it's time for you to start collecting information.

*After you've broken the ice, you can start collecting information to tailor your sales approach to the client's needs.*

You might be tempted to rush into speaking about your product or service. However, it is of the utmost importance that your client reveals information about his needs first, so that you can then provide solutions.

If you present your information first, your client's guard will be up. Also, you will have no way to tailor your conversation to what the client is really seeking. If you are a financial planner, and you talk about everything from life insurance to annuities and investments, you might turn off the person who simply wants to set up a college fund.

You can uncover most of your clients' needs by asking a series of questions. However, even in a warmed-up relationship, clients may keep their needs somewhat to themselves. It's not that they don't want to share with you; it's simply that people are automatically guarded during the sales process. They don't want to feel sold. This is why it's important to lead your customers to discover a need for your product or service on their own.

Don't be afraid to open with one of the simplest questions possible. It might make you feel as if you sound underprepared, but it will launch you in the direction you need to head.

"So, why are we meeting today?"

*Get clients talking about their needs.*

This likely will make you feel awkward, and it might do the same to your client. They're used to hearing sales pitches almost as soon as they hear hello. Depending on the industry, you can ask that question in a variety of ways. The main idea is to get the customer talking about her needs. Once you get the ball rolling, the idea is to keep asking the right questions until you lead the client into asking for your specific product or service. You must remember at all times that—contrary to what your sales manager tells you—you may not always have what someone needs. Remember to keep the line of questioning focused on your client and her needs. Stay as far away as possible from talking about yourself or your own product for as long as you can.

Let's follow a simple line of questioning for a used-car salesman while investigating a few detours along the way. Carl will be selling a car to Beth.

**Carl:** So what brings you in today?

**Beth:** Well, I'm looking for a car.

**Carl:** Okay! What's the purpose of the car?

**Beth:** It's for my daughter's graduation.

Notice how Carl didn't go right for, "What kind of car are you looking for?" He set out to find the purpose of the car. By defining what his client needs as opposed to her self-assessed solution, he's taking the right steps.

Having the core reason for this purchase helps Carl direct the sale and begins to build the need within his client. This isn't just another car; it's a car for her daughter, who has accomplished something. There is a more emotional connection to the sale already being created.

**Carl:** That's great—congratulations! What are your daughter's plans with this car? Is she going off to college or entering the workforce?

**Beth:** She's actually moving 2,000 miles away from home to go to school in Utah!

Again, Carl didn't ask, "What kind of car does she want?" In his mind, he's been able to narrow down the type of car and build a case for his initial suggestions.

**Carl:** Wow, that's quite a ways away! What made her choose to go to school out there?

**Beth:** They've got a great program for her major, but our budget really directed a good part of her school search.

Now, with a question totally unrelated to the actual car, Carl has learned more about the overall purchase situation, and he can back up the suggestion he's about to make.

**Carl:** Well, I have a few ideas for you. This is obviously going to be a long move for your daughter, so room and safety are big factors. An SUV might cover those needs, but with a budget in mind, I have some really nice, sporty wagons you might want to look at. They're safe, roomy, and a little bit better on the purchase price and gas budget than an SUV will be. Plus, some of the sportier late-model wagons we have on the lot are much sharper than the station wagon you might be envisioning.

Carl listened to all of Beth's needs and desires for her daughter's car purchase and then used them to make an initial suggestion. Beth shared enough information that she can build a bond with the idea, and Carl earned her trust by truly starting the sale in her best interests. A roomier wagon is a perfect idea for a budget-minded move. Carl also knew that, by default, safety would be a concern, and he even addressed any image concerns that might come along with driving a wagon.

But for a moment, let's assume that Carl did not keep the questions personal and instead started off by cutting right to the chase.

**Carl:** So, what kind of car are you looking for?

**Beth:** I'd like to keep the budget right around $12,000.

**Carl:** Well, the best value would be a subcompact car that's last year's model.

Beth might have been led along to look at a little two-door car. It's nice and updated but lacking any room, so she immediately will write off the idea. Carl didn't do anything wrong, but he also didn't get to the bottom of Beth's needs. Sure, she might tell him she's looking for more room or something else, but why not establish those needs immediately? What if she was only stopping in on her lunch break, and she immediately decides to check out another place tomorrow? What has Carl done to show he cares about the purchase she's considering making?

# Uncovering Client Needs

This line of questioning lends to a needs-based selling process. The most important step of the sales process, after prospecting, is uncovering your clients' needs.

For you to secure a sale, your client must have a need for your product or service. He may have an idea of what his need is, but it is your job to amplify this through your line of questioning. When you solidify an existing need, your product or service will virtually sell itself.

The remaining sales process from this point on is a moot point if you don't uncover your clients' needs. Having these needs in hand will help you with each and every remaining step of the sales process.

Make sure you master all of these opening techniques, and the rest of your sales process will be a cinch!

# Action Plan

✓ Use news sources to stay on top of local news and happenings.

✓ If your sales process is long enough, research any clients with whom you have an upcoming meeting.

✓ Think about some of your hobbies and experiences that you can use to relate to your clients on a personal level.

✓ Think about people you've met and the style of communication they would best relate to.

✓ Consider the typical sales questions your peers ask their clients. Can you change those questions just enough to get a more personal response?

✓ Determine what kinds of questions will direct clients toward your product or service.

# Chapter 4

# Presentation, Solutions, and Recommendations

- Stock Presentations
- Marketing Materials
- Pricing
- Presentation Tactics
- Recommendations
- Agreement
- Nonessential Products and Services
- Average and Better Case Studies
- Action Plan

The most familiar phase of the sales process is the presentation. This is when it's generally accepted that a salesperson is doing all of his "selling." The salesperson presents features and benefits of the product or service, and the client is so utterly impressed that she can't say no.

If only it were that simple, we'd all be replaced by fact sheets and video demonstrations. In reality, your client must be sold before you even reach this step. In the previous chapter, we talked about uncovering your clients' needs. If you've discovered that your client needs a Phillips-head screwdriver and that it will be the solution to his current situation, you have to do little more than simply present one on a pillow.

Of course, most products or services requiring a salesperson are a little more complex than the screwdriver example. The point I'm trying to drive home is that the presentation process will be fruitless if you haven't uncovered a need or want that you can solve with your product or service.

## Stock Presentations

Memorize stock presentations until they are so second-nature that they no longer sound canned and rehearsed.

Shortly after you start your sales position, you'll be drilled on your company's tried-and-true presentation. You'll have to recite each and every feature and benefit until you're blue in the face so that the company can rest assured that you won't leave anything out. As robotic and canned as this may seem, it is important that you memorize these materials. Memorize them so well that it doesn't seem as if you've memorized them at all. If you can get comfortable enough, the information will flow freely and won't sound quite as canned as it did on day one.

Most importantly, memorizing this information will let you customize the presentation process to meet your customers' needs. When you can do so effectively, presentations will morph into a "solutions" phase in your sales process. By trimming and directing the stock presentation your company has provided on a case-by-case basis, you'll have better results in your sales career. How many times have you been on the other side of the table from a salesperson who is about to begin her presentation and thought, "Here we go...?" Turning your presentation into a solution will streamline this step and make the process more comfortable for everyone involved.

# Marketing Materials

Your company will provide you with countless marketing pieces that speak to any number of features and benefits of your product or service. These tools can be useful for solidifying specific points, but drowning your client in information will often dampen your presentation's effectiveness. Become very familiar with any marketing pieces you might consider using in your presentation or leaving with your client, so that you can tailor which pieces you present to any given customer.

The number-one pitfall of using marketing materials is most evident when a salesperson does not take the time to master the information. Many salespeople use these materials as a supplement to their own knowledge. They use marketing materials to fill in the blanks instead of to support their recommendations. Truth be told, if you don't know the ins and outs of what you're suggesting, you're doing your customer a disservice by relying on a piece of paper to make your points.

*Know the information in your marketing materials and integrate it into your sales presentations.*

Use marketing materials to stress the most important points of your presentation. Consider the way a homeowner's insurance salesperson might present his marketing materials when suggesting flood coverage:

> "Not every homeowner elects to purchase flood insurance. Many do not need it. However, when we spoke earlier, you were concerned about your basement being below the waterline of the Blue River, less than a quarter mile from your home. I have a fact sheet about flooding in your area over the past 50 years. Based on these numbers, the Blue River floods approximately every 16 years. If you plan on living in your home for several years, flood insurance makes sense."

This may have been a bit of a simplified example, but the salesperson integrated the marketing piece he was going to leave with the customer. How could someone mix up such an easy example? It's simple:

> "I know you're a little worried about flooding, so here's some information on flooding and the Blue River."

In the second example, the salesperson made no attempt to explain the relevance of the information or even point out the parts that supported his recommendation. Based simply on these two snippets of conversation, which client is more likely to say yes when the salesperson offers her flood insurance?

# Pricing

If it's not already clear by this point, pricing can be one of the most difficult parts of the presentation for both the salesperson and the client. Everything looks great when your customer can have his needs met and you can be the one providing all of the solutions. However, these feelings can change when price comes into the picture.

There are many ways to deal with pricing, according to whom you ask in the sales world. Some people will tell you to fight tooth and nail to get out every single feature and benefit before you drop the pricing bomb on your customer. In some ways, they're right—if your client doesn't fully realize what she's getting, she may focus more on sticker shock than on listening to the rest of your presentation.

Other sales professionals will tell you to let the pricing fly. If someone wants to cut you short with, "How much?" then have at it. Your product is so great that it doesn't matter what it costs or when the customer finds out the price! This is one of the less popular stances on pricing, but you can learn a lot by giving it some thought. If you hold off on your pricing and make it a big secret until the end of your presentation, it will turn into the biggest and most crucial point of the presentation. Being a little looser with revealing price downplays its epic importance to the entire transaction.

Hold off on telling a customer the price for as a long as *naturally* possible.

In my experience, holding off on the price for as long as *naturally* possible works best. If your customer wants to cut to the chase and seems adamant about doing so, you have to let it go. Otherwise, get through your entire presentation. If you let go of the pricing too soon, your presentation will be focused on qualifying the cost. If you keep it until the end, your presentation will be focused on providing the customer with solutions to the needs you've previously uncovered.

Here's an example:

> "Our monthly landscaping service is $195. It might be more than others out there, but we use top-of-the-line products for seeding and fertilization. We also have some of the most experienced landscapers in the market, and we pay them well to keep them around."

Letting price go early, the salesperson felt obligated to qualify it by pointing out why her service is a little more costly than that of the competition. Now consider this approach:

> "Our high-quality products will take care of the bald patches you've been so concerned with in the yard. Between the products and our highly experienced staff, we'll have no problem improving your yard and managing the general upkeep of your landscaping. The monthly fee for this service is just $195."

The second salesperson used the features and benefits to address the client's needs, as opposed to qualifying the price of the service.

## Presentation Tactics

If you haven't already figured it out, I'm not a huge fan of sales tricks and gimmicks. There is no magical way to present your product that will get everyone to buy. That being said, you can follow some professional tactics and ideas to improve the effectiveness of your presentation.

Just to beat a dead horse one more time, the presentation process is almost a moot point if you don't uncover needs that you can meet during the initial discovery phase of the sales process. Everything about the recommendations you make *must* be tied into your clients' needs.

Depending on how long your sales process is, it's best to attempt to make the transition to your presentation a seamless process. If you can master this skill, your solutions will seem less abrupt, and your client will be more open to hearing you out. In a longer sales process, the presentation phase will be an obvious and stand-alone event. Even still, you can make the way you open it seem less intrusive.

The transition from discovering your client's needs to making your sales presentation should be as seamless as possible.

Let's first consider a short sales process. We'll start with an example of a bumpy transition by an insulation salesperson:

> "It seems pretty clear that reducing your heating costs is important to you. Okay, let me tell you about our insulation services. We have been in business since 1929. We use the most efficient insulating products available."

It's abrupt, right? Now consider a smooth transition:

> "It's clear that reducing your heating costs is important to you, and that's really what we've been doing for more than 80 years. The products we use will help address your heating costs immediately."

In the first example, you can see clearly where the salesperson wraps up the fact-finding and begins the presentation. In the second example, the salesperson is more conversational and blends the two steps together. You can see that he's already on track for a customized presentation. The first salesperson's client is likely leaning back in her chair and getting comfortable for a long presentation.

Now let's consider a long sales process. We'll start with a bumpy opening by an investment advisor:

> "Thank you for taking the time to meet with me again. I know a little bit about you and your needs, and now I want to tell you more about us and how we can help you reach your financial goals. Our firm was one of the few in the area to navigate the recent recession well...."

Now consider a smooth opening:

> "Thank you for taking the time to meet with me again. It was clear to me that you were concerned with weathering any future turbulence in the market, so I have some ideas that will take advantage of our firm's strong financial history."

In the long sales process, it's a little more evident that a presentation is going to take place, as it's often the sole purpose of a particular meeting. Even so, the second example demonstrates a more natural start to a conversation. In the first example, the client is likely ready for the salesperson to start flipping through a binder of facts and marketing materials. The second salesperson is more likely to have a natural conversation, with the occasional marketing piece slid across the table to punctuate a point.

# Recommendations

After the presentation is comfortably opened, it's time to make your recommendations. No matter what you suggest, you must tie it back to your customers' needs. (There's that dead horse again!) If what you're suggesting doesn't meet any of your customer's defined wants or needs, you're trying to sell ice to an Eskimo. Also, make sure you inform the customer of how your product or service will fit his previously discussed wants or needs. Don't assume he'll make the connection on his own.

> Always tie your recommendations into the customer's needs.

Here's an example:

> "Based on what you're looking for, I feel that our SuperTech3400 phone would best suit your needs."

This salesperson may have suggested the right phone, but he offered no reasoning. There may be an opportunity to explain, but why risk it? Instead, try something like this:

> "Based on the fact that you'd like touchscreen ability and a high-resolution camera, the SuperTech3400 would best meet your needs."

This salesperson restated the customer's need and connected it to his recommendation.

The most important part of this stage is that you recommend something that will fill your clients' needs. This is the point where we separate professional salespeople from con artists. If you sell people things that make sense and will perform as stated, you'll be able to sleep at night, and you'll close more sales in the long run. If you try to falsely meet your clients' needs with unnecessary products or services, it will catch up with you in the long run.

# Agreement

It's important to get continual agreement throughout your presentation. When you make any kind of point or connection, make sure your client is in agreement. This can help you in a variety of ways.

> Remember to get continual agreement from your client throughout your presentation.

First, it will allow you to address any questions before completing your recommendations. If there is an issue or you missed the point of the customer's need, addressing it immediately is better than ending the sales call with a big, fat no.

Second, continual agreement lends to overall agreement. If your client has agreed on nine or ten points you've made and facts you've pointed out in relation to her needs, she is far more likely to be in agreement when you ask for her business.

# Nonessential Products and Services

Leave the door open for future sales of products or services without pushing nonessential ones at the current time.

It is important to direct your solutions and recommendations to your clients' needs, but there is nothing wrong with mentioning other products to plant the seeds for later transactions. You may not be able to sell them to your client right away, but if he knows they exist and he's happy with his first experience, a later sale will come much more easily.

Suppose a copier sales and service person is called in simply to provide a small law firm with a high-volume copier for basic office needs. Without selling the service on the spot, the salesperson could easily plant the seed for a later transaction.

"The CopyKat800 will certainly fill your needs for reliability and a low-maintenance machine. The other great thing is that it is compatible with our individual desk scanners. If you ever want to give your attorneys the ability to scan a document directly to the printer, it will be a seamless transition."

Here, the salesperson didn't directly sell the secondary service, but she gave herself a reason to call again at a later date. However, directly selling the scanners immediately, without the customer verbalizing any need, can alienate clients and possibly even ruin a sale. For example:

"The CopyKat800 will certainly fill your needs for reliability and a low-maintenance machine. I'm also suggesting six of our desktop scanners, because I imagine your attorneys need to scan and copy contracts all the time."

In this example, the salesperson made a decent assumption but asked for the business based on nothing but a hunch. In doing so, she may have alienated a client.

# Average and Better Case Studies

This section provides some examples of typical presentations. There's nothing necessarily *wrong* with the first example in each case study, but the second example displays a better approach based on what we've talked about in this chapter.

## Case Study 1

Name: Devin

Industry: Home security

Client: Mr. Henderson

Business/consumer: Homeowner

Here's an example of a normal presentation:

**Devin:** Thank you for taking the time to meet with me again. I took a look at your needs, and I have some good ideas for you. We're one of the most reliable home security companies in the nation. Clients using our service get a much better response rate than those using most of our competitors' services. Here is a sheet with more information on this.

**Mr. Henderson:** Thanks. How much is this going to cost?

**Devin:** Well, it's $79 per month with a $299 startup fee, but it's well worth the investment. We have local operators available, and the equipment we use is top of the line; it even has a backup power source.

**Mr. Henderson:** Can I get a cheaper model?

**Devin:** You can. Let me check my price list....

Devin started off his presentation by speaking right to the features and benefits of his product. Regardless of whether it met Mr. Henderson's needs, he didn't make the connection or even ask for confirmation. He had a great marketing piece, but he didn't put it to its best use. Because Devin immediately gave the price when he was asked, the entire conversation switched to cost and managing the price.

Here are some slight modifications that could help Devin close the sale:

**Devin:** Thank you for taking the time to meet with me again. I know one of your biggest concerns was response time from our emergency call center. Is that still the case?

**Mr. Henderson:** Certainly.

**Devin:** I pulled this information sheet from our database. It compares our response time to that of the two other major competitors in the area. As you can see, we beat them by an average of two minutes and twenty seconds. A pretty big chunk of time, wouldn't you agree?

**Mr. Henderson:** Wow, that's a pretty big difference! How much is this going to cost?

**Devin:** Well, the price is pretty competitive considering what you get. Our local call center has a lot to do with the quick response time. When you couple that with our hardware and its backup power source, our competition simply cannot compete.

Devin made just a few changes to his presentation to increase his odds of a sale. As soon as he opened, he tied his client's needs into the conversation and got confirmation. He used his marketing piece to make a point, but he went into depth about the pertinent content. Again, Devin sought out agreement. When Mr. Henderson asked about price, Devin somewhat rolled over it, because it didn't seem as if Mr. Henderson was cutting to the chase. Devin spoke of the remaining features and benefits to make it clear that his company could address Mr. Henderson's needs better than the competition could. If price came up again, Devin would have already made his case for meeting Mr. Henderson's needs, and the price would not have to be qualified.

## Case Study 2

Name: Sandra

Industry: Direct mail

Client: Mrs. Clark

Business/consumer: Foundation construction and repair

Here's an example of a normal presentation:

> **Sandra:** Thank you for meeting with me again, Mrs. Clark. I know you're concerned with reaching out to affluent home-owners, so I brought you some helpful marketing information on our company. Here's a basic fact sheet about our company, our mission statement, some of our ad sizes, some information about the different ZIP codes, and some testimonials from our current customers.
>
> **Mrs. Clark:** Wow, that's a lot of stuff. I don't have a lot of time to go through all of this. How much will it cost me to do a mailing with you?
>
> **Sandra:** Don't worry; I'll get to that. You're going to love our product and love our price! We've been helping other business owners just like you reach out to homeowners for more than 20 years. We…
>
> **Mrs. Clark:** Listen, I just want the price.
>
> **Sandra:** Okay! I'll cut to the chase. Ten thousand mailings every month to the ZIP code of your choice, plus our exclusive web and email services, which will help you get even more customers, will cost $1,399 per month.
>
> **Mrs. Clark:** Web and email?!

Sandra was crashing right from the beginning. She overloaded her client with countless marketing pieces that didn't seem to pertain to her business needs. Right away, Mrs. Clark wanted to cut to the pricing. Sandra rolled over the first request but hyped up the service and price too much as she moved on to her canned presentation. When Mrs. Clark demanded the price again, Sandra gave in but overloaded her recommendation with things she'd never qualified to Mrs. Clark.

Here is a better approach for Sandra:

> **Sandra:** Thank you for meeting with me again, Mrs. Clark. I know you were concerned with reaching out to affluent homeowners, so I pulled the demographics for people owning homes built before 1970 with incomes of more than $150,000 annually. Would you say that identifies your top customers based on income and the likely need for foundation repair?

**Mrs. Clark:** It certainly does! How much will it cost to mail to these homes?

**Sandra:** Based on our bulk-mailing rate, it's 8.9 cents per home. We can adjust how many homes we hit or play with the demographics a bit to work within your budget. Further down the road, we could also retarget many of these clients using a follow-up email system.

**Mrs. Clark:** Okay, so $890 for 10,000 homes? That's not bad. Let's start with that, and then maybe we'll try the email thing later.

Sandra did so well in the second instance that she didn't even need to actively close. She immediately tied in the client's need with one highly thought-out fact sheet. After getting agreement, she was asked about price. Instead of fully rolling over the issue, she gave the individual price per mailing to ease Mrs. Clark into the full price. Also, Sandra did a great job at planting the seed for a future service without forcing it down her client's throat.

Fact finding and uncovering your clients' needs is crucial to the sales process. If you complete that step correctly, the presentation phase will turn into a solutions and recommendations session with your client. Closing is just one step (and one chapter) away.

# Action Plan

✓ Learn about the presentation scripts and dialogue your company has made available to its sales force. Memorize this format and information!

✓ Consider what sort of marketing materials you can use to back up your sales.

✓ Make sure you're comfortable with these marketing materials.

✓ Practice making a smooth transition into your presentation before you meet with your client.

✓ Without up-selling on the spot, think about the seeds you can plant with your clients for future sales calls and transactions.

✓ Consider what specific needs you uncovered with your client initially (if any) and how your company can provide solutions.

# Chapter 5

# Closing

More books have been written about closing than about any other part of the sales process. Some people consider asking for the sale the most difficult part of sales. Some find that mastering this process is the sign of a true salesman. Many sales managers will stress this as the most important step in the process. However, if you haven't already figured out my stance on this step, you've likely been skimming the book.

Prospecting is the most important and most difficult part of sales. Closing is the easiest part of sales—well, the easiest part next to cashing your paycheck. However, it's the easiest part of sales if and only if you lay the proper groundwork. When you uncover your client's needs and address them with your solutions at a reasonable rate, the closing is almost automatic. If you do your job correctly, your client more often than not will be the one closing the sale.

The main purpose of this chapter is to get critics and sales managers to recommend this book simply because there is a chapter on closing…. In all seriousness, this chapter should be titled, "How Not to Mess Up the Close." The business is yours for the taking if you bring the right client with the right needs to the right product or service with the right solutions.

However, even if you perfectly navigate the opening, fact-finding, and presentation stages of the sales process, there is still room for you to blow your sale. The following sections cover some ways your sale could come crashing down.

## Pushing Away the Sale

Pushing away a sale is one of the most common ways a sale can fall apart.

This seems like one of the most obviously counterproductive moves you could make in the world of sales. Surprisingly, it's one of the most common ways a sale can fall apart.

People like to move toward the path of least resistance. When the sales process comes to an end, the most easy and comfortable close for an untrained salesperson is to advise her customer to put off his decision until another time. If you're new to the world of sales, this might seem odd, but if you've been in the industry for a while, you may have seen or experienced this paradox.

Every step of the process is complete. Questions have been asked and answered, presentations have been made, and the price is out there.

> "Okay, now, think it over, and we'll touch base again in a week or so."

Requesting no answer can sometimes feel easier than asking for an answer. Sometimes the emotional risk of hearing "no" outweighs the benefit of hearing yes. Whatever the reason, you must fight the desire to default the decision to another day. There will be many instances in sales where people do, in fact, need time to think things over, but don't offer to give them more time simply for the sake of taking the easy way out of the close.

You may feel a sense of accomplishment at getting the sales process over with, but that accomplishment doesn't pay the bills. There is a time and a way to ask for the sale, but avoiding it greatly increases the chances of a delayed "no."

## Closing Too Hard

The opposite of the previous example will yield similar results. Some sales managers will teach you how to search for buying signals and how to strike at the perfect time to find the close. They want you to focus on sniffing out these signals and closing instantly. Others will tell you to never leave the final meeting without a yes or a no. A small fraction will even encourage you to use pressure or guilt to finalize the sale.

Some of these tactics may work. Some might get you more sales or shorten your sales process. But in reality, these coercive moves that may get you some immediate results are no way to build a real sales career.

Buying signals are great. They mean that you're on track, and your customer is interested. However, that doesn't mean the customer doesn't need to go through some version of your sales process. If someone comes into an auto dealership and says, "I've got to have that car," the next step isn't simply to say, "Sign here." You still have to work through your customer's needs to solidify the sale. There may be a few times when the customer would sign for the car on the spot, but more than likely, she'd come to her senses before making such a spur-of-the-moment decision. Sure, she wants the car, but have you uncovered her need? Let's look at an example.

Even if your customer is giving you buying signals, you still need to take him through the sales process.

**Rod:** That's the most beautiful sports car I've ever seen. I'll take it!

**Andy:** Perfect! Let me get the paperwork ready.

**Rod (after reviewing the paperwork):** Wow, that's a little more expensive than I bargained for. The gas mileage is terrible, too. Maybe I should think this over.

Andy acted on the first buying signal and did nothing to secure the sale. He closed far too early and didn't complete the sales process. Let's see whether Beth can take a crack at the same situation.

**Rod:** That's the most beautiful sports car I've ever seen. I'll take it!

**Beth:** I know. Isn't she a beauty? What's the occasion?

**Rod:** The occasion? I want that car!

**Beth:** That's great! Is it for you or your family, or is it your second car?

**Rod:** No, I want it for myself. I've worked hard all my life, and I'd like to treat myself to something new and exciting.

**Beth:** Great! So you want an exciting car as a sort of gift to yourself for a life of hard work?

**Rod:** Absolutely!

Rod obviously wants the car. He did, in fact, give a strong and obvious buying signal. Beth solidified the sale by using the buying signal to bring out his needs. Now this sale will come to a more natural close.

It's important for Beth to keep feeding this need throughout the remainder of the sales process. When they go for the test drive, Beth can focus on what a "treat" this car is and how car enthusiasts purchase it for its exciting performance. Rod's need will continue to solidify, giving less credence to objections that may come up later, such as cost or poor gas mileage. In the case of the objections rearing their heads, Beth can remind Rod that the car isn't about economy; it's about the rewards of owning a fine sports car.

In addition to abusing early buying signals, a salesperson can ruin the sale by applying too much pressure. People have grown used to and tired of hearing certain sales phrases deployed to ensure a close. It takes them out of their comfort zone and causes them to raise their natural defenses to "being sold." Have you ever cringed when you've been on the other side of these sales phrases? Did you ever feel what I generally feel about these statements?

"This price is good today only. Tomorrow, we go back to the original pricing."

Really? Your profit margins fluctuate that often, and this is it?

"If you don't want this, I've got another guy coming in this afternoon looking for the same thing."

Then why are you so worried about selling it to me?

"Let me talk to my manager and see whether we can work something out."

So what you're saying is that you build wiggle room into the price, and I'm supposed to trust you?

"Look, I'm not even making any money on this deal now. I just want you to send your friends in to do business with me."

I would never send my friends in to see someone who clearly just lied to me.

"You can't make this decision on your own? Do you have to run it by your spouse every time you want to use the bathroom?"

Wow—does that *ever* work?!

Even *if* these gimmicky pressure tactics work, you have three things to look forward to: A chargeback because your client canceled your product or service, *no* future business from that client, and *no* future referrals.

## Talking Past the Sale

This issue can kill a sale at close, but it's usually an underlying issue throughout the entire sales process. After every step has been completed, and the salesperson has stated the price, he just keeps talking—and talking and talking and talking.

Similar to the first issue that can ruin a close—pushing it away— salespeople sometimes want to avoid the decision-making step to the process. They're so nervous that when the price is out there, they don't want an answer, and they feel as if they must overqualify the price they've just delivered.

If you've gone through the sales process effectively, there is no need to keep talking to qualify the price you've just delivered.

59

Here is an all-too-common example:

> "…and the final price on this television is $2,499. Now, I know that might seem like a lot, but remember, it has high-definition picture and sound, and it can be hooked up to your wireless network. You don't have to set it up, because, as I said, we'll install it for you. If you don't like it, you can always return it within 60 days, but I'm sure you'll like it because of all these great features and.…"

And so on. The customer was likely sold already—maybe even before the price was made into an issue. However, this verbose salesperson may have caused the consumer's guard to shoot back up. The customer might think, "Why is this guy so nervous? Why won't he shut up? Is he pulling a fast one on me? Something's not right."

Of course, this may not kill every sale, but it might cause concern for someone who's on the fence. You might even bring up a point that the customer never considered.

> "Oh, this is compatible with my home wireless network? I don't need that, so let me look at something cheaper."

That fact should have been uncovered already, early on in the sales process. Now you've started the sales process all over again, and the potential customer might not trust you as much anymore.

# Psychological Failure

There is a bit of psychology at play during the closing process. It certainly plays somewhat of a role throughout the entire sales process, but this is where it shows through the most and can have the heaviest effect on the outcome.

*If you're not confident about yourself or your product, your customer won't be either.*

If you come across as extremely passive and unsure of yourself or your product or services, your customers will feel the same way. They'll think you're not sold on your own sale and that they should therefore stay away.

Here is an example of a negative salesperson's close. Peter is shifting and slouching in his seat. His voice is quiet, and when he can be heard, his dialogue is filled with self-conscious terms such as, "Uh."

"I really think our carpets are the best, but, uh, the price for your first floor is $3,450. I know that's a lot but, I mean, it includes installation. You don't have to do it, but that's the price."

Anyone who actually talks like that isn't likely to get hired in the first place, but I think you can see where I'm going with this extreme example. If you have doubt in your product or service, so will your customer.

The opposite is also true. If you come across as extremely arrogant and sure of your product beyond any reasonable expectations, people won't trust you, and they'll treat you like a stereotypical salesperson. Here is an example arrogant salesperson's close:

"Look, our carpets are the best in town. Our competitors' are garbage, and anyone with half a brain is doing business with us. Not that the price should even matter, but this is going to cost you $3,450. When do we start?"

This guy isn't putting any of his potential clients at ease. First of all, his arrogance is nauseating. Second, being competitive is good, but shredding the competition makes you look unprofessional. You never know whether your client may have had a past relationship with the company you're badmouthing and knows that what you're saying is false. Also, in the same sentence, this salesperson implied that his customer would have less than half a brain if he says no! To top it off, he used an assumptive close on his customer. This is when you assume the answer is yes and say something like, "When do you want to start?" or, "Will it be cash, check, or charge?" This is a bit of a gimmick that may work from time to time, but not after the display leading up to this example!

# Effective Closing

If the aforementioned are ways to screw up the closing, what's the right way to close a sale? It's a fair question, considering that we focused on the wrong way to close a sale first. Truly, the best way to close a sale is a simple one that avoids any of the aforementioned pitfalls. If you've established and met a need and offered a reasonable price, the sale will (almost) naturally come to a close.

> When the need is met and a reasonable price is offered, the sale will come to a natural close.

Sometimes a close can be as simple as asking the customer what she thinks about your proposal. Other times you can just pause and wait for a response. What's key to remember is that there is no magical phrase that will make your customer automatically say yes. Some sales training focuses so hard on the closing process that they imply you can close anyone, no matter how poor the rest of the process, if you just use the right tactics. These kinds of "closer" tactics keep the salesman stigma alive. If you haven't convinced your client that you can meet his needs, it doesn't matter how many tricks you have up your sleeve. And in the off chance that a trick works, there is still no benefit in the long run.

Direct your customer to offer a buying decision.

Realistically, you'll need to direct your customer to offer up her buying decision. Some will take the mention of a price as your close and simply say yes or no. Others will need a bit of coaxing to realize that the process is coming to a close. Some will offer up objections but simply need some answers and settling so they can make a decision. Here are several examples of how you can close a sale.

Veronica is selling web-design services to Wayne, a home builder. Let's assume she uncovered her client's needs and made a recommendation that provided the right solution.

## Closing 1

**Veronica:** …and this is why I'm certain our design services will deliver the website your business needs. The final price for these services is $6,500.

**Wayne:** That sounds like a fair price. Let's do it.

Remember, some sales will simply fall into place with the proper moves made up to this point.

## Closing 2

**Veronica:** …and this is why I'm certain our design services will deliver the website your business needs. The final price for these services is $6,500.

**Wayne:** That sounds like a fair price.

**Veronica:** Great! So should we go ahead and get started?

**Wayne:** Sure.

Almost as easy as the first example, except Veronica simply had to ask for the sale.

## Closing 3

**Veronica:** ...and this is why I'm certain our design services will deliver the website your business needs. The final price for these services is $6,500.

**Wayne:** That sounds reasonable. Let me think it over.

**Veronica:** I'm sure this may take some time to digest. If you're feeling a little hesitant, is there anything I can clear up for you to help make this decision process easier?

Veronica isn't applying any unneeded pressure. However, she wants to make sure that any of Wayne's unanswered questions are addressed. She knows that if the sales process went perfectly, there wouldn't be much left to think about. This will give Wayne the chance to voice any concerns that may be holding up the sale. There is a chance that he will say yes or no after his concerns are addressed, but there is a chance he might still elect to take some time to think things over.

## Closing 4

**Veronica:** ...and this is why I'm certain our design services will deliver the website your business needs. The final price for these services is $6,500. How does that sound to you?

**Wayne:** It's a little more than your competitors are charging.

**Veronica:** Besides the pricing, how do our services compare, line by line?

There are two differences with this close. After giving the price, Veronica asks for a response. Some salespeople prefer to simply stop after they've made the price known. Others will use a simple directive to coax a buying decision. This time, Wayne met Veronica with an objection. We will cover objections in a later chapter, but it's important to recognize that this is when objections often surface. Veronica has directed the conversation into a comparison of services, knowing (hoping) that her higher price is qualified by more and better services.

## Closing 5

**Veronica:** ...and this is why I'm certain our design services will deliver the website your business needs. The final price for these services is $6,500.

**Wayne:** Veronica, you've been very helpful and informative, but this is simply something we cannot do at this time.

**Veronica:** May I ask whether there is something you didn't like about our product, service, or price?

**Wayne:** No, it's all great; it's just not something we're going to do at this time.

Remember, even the best salesperson can't sell everyone everything. You might find and address your clients' needs at a better than fair price, and they may choose not to do business with you. No matter how well you do, you must be prepared to hear no in your closing. Veronica did decide to ask whether there was anything that held up the sale. It can be a great learning experience to find out why you weren't a fit, and once in a great while, it may open up a conversation that leads to a yes. It's up to you how far you push the questioning, because you never know when your client may want to do business in the future or refer others down the road.

# Problematic Closing

Some people are chronic non-closers. They may fall prey to some of the pitfalls mentioned earlier. Even after addressing those issues, some people will still have continual problems closing the sale.

Any time I've heard about someone having bad luck with closing, the real problem became evident immediately. Time and time again, I've had co-workers confide in me about their problems with closing. They weren't being pushy; they asked for the sale, and all they got were negative responses or the runaround.

If you don't follow the first two steps in sales of uncovering needs and meeting them with effective recommendations, getting to the close may be virtually impossible. Of course, these salespeople I mentioned were going through the motions, but they were trying to close their clients with the "So what do you want?" approach.

This happened to some of the nicest people I worked with. They'd get an appointment based simply on their good manners and low-pressure attitude. They'd go to their first appointment to build rapport and collect information. A while later, they would go see the customer, give a full stock presentation, and review the rates for various products or services.

As I describe the circumstances to you, I'm sure you can guess where the underlying issues are. These salespeople spent an hour with the customer just talking. They were asking some basic business questions but never really uncovering any needs. Then they went right back to the clients and presented them with all kinds of information. Finally, they played the rate card instead of making any kind of recommendation.

Typically, these types of salespeople are afraid to make suggestions to their clients. They want to cover all the bases and let customers make up their minds on their own. In reality, consumers and business owners rely on salespeople for information and recommendations. Whether they do exactly what you suggest or some other version of it is based on other factors, but you must present them with something if you want to close. Asking, "What can I do for you?" is a great way to open a sales meeting, but it's about the worst way to close one.

The key to a successful closing is everything leading up to the point of closing in your sale.

# Action Plan

✓ If you haven't done so already, uncover your customers' needs.

✓ Make recommendations that will be effective solutions to your clients' needs.

✓ Make sure your pricing is concise and ready to be presented.

✓ Present a recommendation of your own, as opposed to using the "What do you want?" approach.

✓ Make sure you don't fall into the trap of implementing coercive closing tactics in lieu of conducting a full and complete sales process.

✓ Focus on being calm and straightforward with your closing. Present your information and simply ask for the sale.

# Chapter 6

# Objections

- Objections 1 through 19
- Action Plan

Business owners and consumers will throw out objections through the entire sales process. Some are offered up when they are initially prospected for a sales meeting; others never rear their head until you attempt to close the sale. Many of these objections are straightforward, but others may have underlying meanings to consider.

There are no tricks to overcoming objections.

Just as there are no tricks to prospecting, opening, or closing, there are no tricks to overcoming objections. Some sales managers or trainers may teach you to "roll over" certain objections. This is just a fancy way to tell you to ignore your client's questions and concerns. In a high-pressure sales situation, these techniques may work on occasion, but these kinds of divisive tactics won't lead to a long shelf life for your sales career.

There is also a common misconception that all sales objections can be overcome. There is certainly a level of expertise involved in recognizing and addressing objections, but no one out there is batting a thousand at all times. Sometimes people are simply priced out of your product or have no need, or they straight out do not like what you're offering compared to the competition.

Learning to deal with objections is an important part of conducting an effective sales process. Learning to recognize that the sale is non-existent and that it is time to move on comes with experience. Remember to keep prospecting at all times so that you can respond to continual objections with, "NEXT!"—in more constructive terms, of course.

This chapter covers some of the most common objections you will come across in sales. It is extremely important to realize that sometimes what the customer is saying is *exactly* what he means!

# Objection 1

"It's too expensive."

## What They're Really Saying

Assuming your product is at least within ballpark range of your competition, most price objections are tied in to quality expectations. This objection generally boils down to two things. First, the customer might be looking for the lowest price regardless of quality. You could completely convince her of your stellar quality, but that's not going to cut it if your price can be beat.

If rock-bottom price isn't what she's looking for, calling something too expensive means that the customer feels there isn't enough value behind the price your product or service is going for. Within this group, a select few of the negotiating type may have voiced this objection just to see whether you lower your price.

## How to Respond

If it's a matter of pure price, and you have no room to negotiate, there isn't much you can do. This is why the first step in overcoming this objection is to determine whether it is really about price or lack of assumed value. Don't be afraid to deal with an objection with a straightforward question or response.

> "Are you shopping around for the lowest price, or do you feel that my product or service isn't worth the investment?"

This type of response helps you quickly direct the rest of your sales conversation. In addition to finding out whether your potential client is a shopper, this can also bring the negotiators to the surface.

Remember, people who truly find your price too high will mentally check out of the sales process. There's no more room for back and forth in their minds. The negotiators will continue to declare that it's too expensive, yet they will show a continued interest. Some might come right out and ask you whether there is anything you can do with the price, or they may even offer up their own version of a suggested retail value. How you choose to deal with someone who wants to negotiate is up to you and your pricing control.

The group of individuals who haven't been convinced of quality are the ones you have the most room to work with. This doesn't mean that they need to hear each and every feature and benefit again, though. Start to pull out the very specific features and benefits that are holding them up from making a sales decision.

> "What about our product isn't up to your standards?"

> "What have you seen in our competition that makes you uncertain about what we're offering?"

These two questions direct your client to bring out the line-item parts of her objection. Now you have the opportunity to speak to the real foundation of her concerns. Expand upon the specifics she is concerned with so that she can determine whether her initial assessment was a bit off. You might also learn that you simply do not have what the customer is looking for.

Know your product inside out so you can be prepared for these situations!

# Objection 2

"I can't afford that right now."

## What They're Really Saying

This objection might sound similar to, "It's too expensive," yet the true meaning generally works out to be a little less favorable for the salesperson.

This is an easier way out for a disinterested client. He's not saying he doesn't like it; he's saying he doesn't have the resources to make the purchase. While this may or may not be true, it's an easier way for the customer to end the sales process. You can't come back right away and ask what he didn't like about the product, because he's claiming the non-sale is based on his own financial restrictions.

## How to Respond

Fortunately, this objection also splits two ways. What the customer has said may be the absolute truth. Find out whether your client eventually wants to make the purchase and when you can contact him to complete the sales process.

"When would be a better time for us to complete this transaction?"

"Can any of our financing or payment plans help to make this less of a strain on your budget?"

This also gives you an opportunity to talk about financing or flexible payment plans if you haven't done so already. Those types of features can help your chances with a client who legitimately does not have the means to make a purchase at this time.

Some more seasoned clientele will use this objection to get out of the sales call, even if it is not the case. They know you can't throw value back at them because it's not what they're debating. People who fall into this category will say things such as, "I'll contact you when I'm ready," or give you a very vague and far-off time to reconnect.

When I've received objections like this in the past, it's clear to me that the sale is likely dead in the water. This is why I've always favored a little bit more of a risky response when it becomes clear I may never hear from the client again.

"If there was anything I could change about the price, features, or benefits, would there be a way we could complete this sales process today?"

You may not be able to change your price. It's even less likely that you can change the features and benefits, depending on the industry you work in. However, this unusual question will either get your customer talking or officially conclude the sales process.

The disinterested will obviously be unmoved and will continue down the path of getting this thing over with. Others may light up about the price. Admitting that an alternative price would make the deal happen locks in the legitimacy of their interest in your product. Now you've gone back to the first objection. The price is too high based on their assessment of its value. Sometimes, they may even skip right to the feature or benefit that is holding up the sale.

Remember, I said that this way of handling the objection can be risky. Asking a question like that implies you have the power to make a change. Keep the conversation on track, but make it clear what powers you actually have over your product or service. Focus on overcoming the root of the customer's objection so that price and affordability are no longer the issue.

If you determine that your client is fully interested and does not have the means to make the transaction at this time, stay on top of whatever timeframe he has given you for conducting business at a later date.

# Objection 3

"I'm not interested."

## What They're Really Saying

Who knows… This is one of the most common stock responses, usually making its appearance during the prospecting phase. It's a very general response, and the customer knows it. It gives you nothing to come back with and makes it very difficult to know where to start.

The short version of the real meaning is, "I don't want to be sold anything, and I don't want to be part of this sales process." It's about as straightforward as it sounds.

The long version of the real meaning is, "You've done nothing to make me interested in your product or service. You have no idea what my needs or wants are, and nothing about our conversation has made it clear to me that you can meet any of them." Harsh, but true. The customer won't be thinking that specifically, but that's what has happened. Nothing about your initial pitch uncovered the customer's desires, and nothing up until the point in the sales process where you've met this objection has offered a way to meet them.

## How to Respond

Although every objection should be handled preemptively if at all possible, none hold more true to that fact than this one.

There are two ways you can handle this objection. First, you can dig and dig in an attempt to find out what you've missed. Using probing questions, you may be able to find out what the customer's real concern is.

The second method, in my opinion, is the best way.

"Okay, thank you for your time!"

Now put down the phone or go back to the office and revisit your personal sales process. Make sure you are prospecting by creating a tangible interest in your product. Make sure you are prospecting to people who *should* be interested in what you have to offer. Make sure you are taking a genuine interest in your clients' needs and providing ways to fill them. When you've perfected that process, the few "I'm not interested" responses you get will be easier to let go.

# Objection 4

"Just send me some info."

## What They're Really Saying

"I'm tired of this process; let's get it over with."

This objection isn't as bad as it sounds. It's likely that your sales process needs some tweaking or that you've gotten a little too verbose, but this sale may still be alive and well. Although the customer is using this as an objection, it actually offers you a great opportunity to uncover his needs.

## How to Respond

"Sure. What would you like to know more about?"

This kind of question will eliminate those using this as a way out of the sale altogether. If they have absolutely no interest, they'll have a hard time answering this question. "I don't know," or, "Whatever" would solidify that notion.

Most will begin to give you all kinds of fodder to build your recommendations, while also giving you the opportunity to keep the conversation going. Remember, this objection generally means the customer is tired of talking to you, so don't push it.

They will always want prices, but do your best to find out what features and benefits they want information on. If warrantees and guarantees are what they're concerned with, you can speak to that during your presentation.

Make sure to set out timelines. Let the customer know what you're going to send, when he should expect it, and when you plan to call on him again. This level of seriousness will be yet another test in determining whether you have a live lead.

# Objection 5

"We're cutting back."

## What They're Really Saying

This is another pricing type of objection. Times may be tough for the customer or for the economy as a whole, and the customer is legitimately concerned with trimming her personal or business budget. When someone lets you know she's cutting back on expenditures, there may still be room for a sale.

This can be an easier objection to overcome, because it's clear that the buyer is making more responsible buying decisions based on her current circumstances. So when a customer tells you, "We're cutting back," she's really saying, "We have to be selective about our purchases, so we're not going to make any impulse purchases."

When the economy is good and people are financially comfortable, it can often take less "selling" to get them to make a purchase. This objection doesn't always mean no; it means you're going to have to work for a bit to get the sale.

## How to Respond

This objection can come up at any point in the sales process, so there are a few different ways to handle it. In general, you have to feature the investment and value features of your product (if there are any available).

A business owner may feel that payroll services should be cut when times are tough. A good payroll representative would help refocus her client to see the investment value.

> "I understand times are tough. Believe it or not, this is why our payroll services can help benefit your business. Think of the man-hours you or your assistant spend compiling and calculating payroll each week. How much is your time worth? Wouldn't it be better spent seeking out and servicing new clients?"

This salesperson qualified the expense against the lost time and money the business would experience from handling payroll on its own.

As another example, even when a consumer is considering cutting back on her cable bill, it's important to address the value and quantify the potential savings.

> "You know, I've had a few customers call in today thinking about canceling their subscription because of the economy. After speaking with them, it made sense to keep their services going after all. Considering the cost of other forms of entertainment, such as movies or dining out, the simple pleasures of television are much more affordable than even one night out on the town."

Although it might sound like a bit of a stretch, the rep does make some good value-based points. Instead of reminding her customer of the thousands of channels to choose from, she focused on the service being a cheap entertainment alternative.

# Objection 6

"I need to talk it over with…"

## What They're Really Saying

"I appreciate your wonderful presentation. Now I'm going to go back to my spouse/partner/friend and simplify all your hard work to, 'Should I buy X for $X?'"

This is another objection that you should deal with before it comes up. It's very important to figure out who all the decision-makers are early on in the sales process to avoid these situations. The fact is, the person you've spent so much time with—building rapport, uncovering needs, and providing solutions—isn't going to do the same with the other decision-maker. He's going to say, "Should we get a new patio for $1,800?" or, "What do you think about upgrading our network for $20,000?"

A $20,000 presentation canned into a single sentence… Although you may do everything you can in advance to avoid this objection, it may still come up.

## How to Respond

"Great, I'm glad you're giving this serious consideration. Do you think it would be possible for me to meet with your husband/wife/associate so that I can present this information to them as well? I think it would make more sense for me to be present just in case any questions arise."

The stated concerns are true, but the purpose of this statement is to prevent your customer from doing a bad job of selling your product or service to the other decision-maker. You need to appeal to both parties' needs, and the only way to do so thoroughly is by direct contact.

Remember, this objection can sometimes turn into a good-cop, bad-cop situation, and you might have to let it go. If you let the customer go back to his partner, he may already be planning on telling you:

> "I *really* want to have you guys install the roof, but my wife wants to go with someone else."

Unfortunately, this guy chose to dump the decision on someone else so he didn't have to feel like the one saying no.

# Objection 7

"I want to think it over."

## What They're Really Saying

> "I'm not totally sold, and I don't want to commit to anything."

This common objection gives your potential client the opportunity to put off making a decision that she's not entirely sure she wants to make. Certainly, some big decisions take time and some mulling over, but you have to ask yourself a question about your product or service: Is the client *really* going to go home and think about everything you just told her? Is she *really* going to sit at her desk and think things over?

In reality, the customer might never think about your sales meeting again until you give her a call to ask her whether she has made a decision. There's also a good chance that she wants to say no, but she's hoping to fade away so she won't have to have a confrontation littered with your attempts to save the sale.

## How to Respond

There is nothing wrong with pointing out the obvious issues with this objection.

> "I'm sure there are some things you need to think over, but I know that may be based on some level of uncertainty. Is there anything that I didn't make entirely clear today or that you would like me to expound upon? I'd hate to have you make a decision without all the necessary details to do so."

This level of openness should coax your client into sharing with you what she may be hung up on. If she doesn't bring any concerns to the table, give her the opportunity to say no so that you can avoid chasing her down later for an answer.

> "Okay, then please feel free to think it over. And don't be afraid to say no. If everyone always said yes, we probably wouldn't even need a sales force!"

Introducing a little levity may put your client at ease and get her to open up to you, or she might even be comfortable enough at that point to say yes or no.

If you give your client the opportunity to think it over, make sure you have a set time to meet or speak again for the decision!

# Objection 8

"Can you do better on the price?"

## What They're Really Saying

> "I'm interested enough, but I want to see whether I can squeeze you for a better deal."

This objection usually leans toward a sales process that will end in a yes. However, this client has seen enough salespeople to know that most will cave immediately if they're holding out on anything. This customer wants to see whether there is any room for negotiating and would feel like a sucker if he didn't at least give it a shot.

## How to Respond

Most customers just throw this objection out there to see whether they can get a deal. They've probably found lower prices or more perks in the past simply by asking. In general, you should be doing your best to give your client exactly what he needs at a standard price, but often you do have room to negotiate or make changes.

Out of fear of losing the sale, many salespeople will immediately offer to cut their commission or cut out some of the particular features or benefits of the deal. Others may attempt to throw other things in to sweeten the deal.

In my opinion, if you do any of these things, your client will lose faith in whatever you've presented. Sure, he might still go ahead and buy, but what you've clearly done is presented him with something flimsy that you're quick to abandon.

> "You know, when I put together this proposal, I factored in all of your needs with our best products and services, along with our best pricing."

Without getting too wordy and sounding nervous, this salesperson stuck to his original plan and displayed his own faith in what he presented.

I would wager to say that this will be enough for most clients. They don't want to get into a big back-and-forth negotiation. For the select few who want to keep going, here are some ideas.

> "Well, I've presented you with what I feel would work best for your needs. Is there some part of this proposal that you see less or no value in?"

This works in two ways. It makes the customer back up his concerns with real content, not just "I want a better price." Also, if changes do in fact need to be made, you've got them right in front of you.

> "Okay, I understand your concerns with the protection plan. If we remove that feature, it saves you $79, but remember, you have to go directly to the manufacturer with any issues you may have."

The sales rep gave room for a cut but made it clear what benefit the client would be losing.

# Objection 9

"I want to wait."

## What They're Really Saying

This is very similar to the "I can't afford it right now" objection. The customer may have found a slight value in what you're offering, but it doesn't fit into the big picture right now for whatever reason. She has not seen the way your solution can fill the needs that you've uncovered.

## How to Respond

The obvious response may be, "Wait for what?" and it might send you down the path of a clearer objection. However, this puts your client on the defensive, and she might feel as if she has to make a case to you about why she is going to wait.

Take some of the needs you uncovered earlier in the process and position them so that waiting might seem like less of a logical option.

> "Well, I understand you may want to wait, but the whole reason we've gotten together is so that we can cut your energy costs with our newest line of windows. I know your energy bills are making you crazy right now, and this is the best way for you to bring them down."

This will either rekindle your customer's sense of urgency or bring out the real, deep-down objection. It might turn out that the customer is getting three other quotes. Finding out about this information will give you a chance to share competitive information and get one more step ahead of your competition. If it was a pricing issue all along, you can go back to some of the earlier pricing objections we discussed.

# Objection 10

"We're happy with our current product or service."

## What They're Really Saying

> "We're happy with our current product or service, *but* if your 30-second speech give us a great reason to change, we might consider it."

People take pride in being loyal to their favorite brands, salespeople, products, services, and so on. It's human nature to have confidence in a decision that you've stuck with for an amount of time, especially if things are going relatively well. If they weren't going well, they might have already called you in the first place.

This objection should be somewhat welcome, as it indicates that the person you've reached out to is familiar and happy with your industry. Play off this important assumption.

## How to Respond

> "That's great! Willy's Window Washing does a good job. But did you know that at Clark's Cleaning, we also pressure-wash our clients' siding for no additional cost?"

This salesperson didn't say anything negative about his competition. He actually praised them! Because the customer clearly has an affinity for his current service, it would be a bad idea to trash someone he appreciates. Very quickly and efficiently, the salesperson noted one of his company's premier features that sets them apart from the competition.

# Objection 11

"I want to shop around."

## What They're Really Saying

This is another two-for-one objection. Some people might mean, "I'm going to shop around and go with the lowest price." They may not 'fess up to such a statement, but it can certainly be fact with some clientele. Unless you are the cheapest place in town, you're not going to get this particular customer.

The ones you are interested in are saying, "Nothing about your product or service wowed me, and I'm going to see what your competition can offer in price and quality." You may still be in the running, but the law of averages would beg to differ. The odds are, someone else will have made evident a better price or service.

Note how I've said "made evident." The truth is, the customer knows only as much as the salesperson informs them of. A person might buy a car from a different dealership because that dealer offered six free carwashes per year. Why didn't the customer buy from your dealership, which offers unlimited carwashes? Because you never told them about it. You can avoid the "I want to shop around" objection by giving a thorough presentation tailored to your customer's needs and wants.

## How to Respond

> "What is it you're hoping to find with the competition?"

This very general question will bring out the basis for the customer's objection. This will break down the objection into a price or quality discussion. If your client is going to be walking away to see the competition, you want to make sure she's fully informed about the specific features and benefits she is concerned with.

If a homeowner is buying furniture from you, she might want to see more of a selection by visiting your competition. If selection is what she wants, maybe sitting down with her and perusing your catalog or website will keep her in the store and help her find exactly what she's looking for. If these customers left the store to find more of a selection, they're likely not going to return.

# Objection 12

"I don't need this."

## What They're Really Saying

"I don't know why I would need this."

Same thing, right? Not quite. If you've been reading with your eyes open, you'll know that uncovering your clients' needs is one of the most important parts of the sales process. There is a very good chance that whoever you are soliciting doesn't need what you're offering, but you'll never know unless you do some digging.

This objection comes up most often when a salesperson leads with the presentation portion of his sales process. "Great to meet you. Let me tell you a little bit about our company...." This objection is the number-one reason why you must uncover your clients' needs *before* you give them a recommendation.

If you lead with a presentation and bog down the customer with all the facts about what you're selling, he can make his own assumption about whether he needs to do business with you.

## How to Respond

If you come across this objection, you have to turn the process upside down and work backward. The verbiage of this specific example could vary greatly from industry to industry, but the idea is the same.

"Okay. So my product wouldn't have any benefit to you or fill any of your needs at all?"

This might sound like a very negative response, but you do want to back out of the process to see whether there's still room for the customer to pull you back in. If he's totally disinterested, then the sale is simply over. However, if there is still life left in it, the customer might conjure up some ways in which the product wouldn't be totally useless.

This negative statement used to back out will make the customer do a little bit of selling the product to himself. As soon as he gives your product any level of credit, start to build upon any of his needs that have shown up. Here is a more linear example:

**Rick:** Okay, so there's nothing our personal trainers could provide for you?

**Sam:** Well, I'm sure they might help me get in better shape, but I don't need a personal trainer.

**Rick:** Are you concerned about getting in better shape?

It seems as if this sales process may be over, but Rick is now getting Sam to focus on a feature that he went out of his way to point out on his own.

# Objection 13

"I heard from X that this is a bad deal."

## What They're Really Saying

Some industries or even specific companies suffer from bad press. It may be actual bad press or just rumors or experiences from friends, family, and colleagues. These are opinions that cannot be ignored, as people don't want to do business with someone who they've been advised to stay away from.

The worst thing you can do is try to discredit what the customer has heard. Showing that *you're* concerned will make the customer feel as if *your company* is also concerned. You will have to learn to defend yourself and your company without attacking the source.

## How to Respond

Ask the customer to expand upon what she has heard. Remind her that you've helped many clients and be honest about any that may have been unhappy. If you sit there and tell the customer that her claim is outrageous and the 100 people you did business with last year are completely satisfied, she won't believe you.

"I can understand your concerns, and believe me, not every carpet installation goes exactly as expected. I worked with about 50 homeowners last year, and most were satisfied. We quickly made good with the handful of clients who experienced a mishap anywhere in the process."

Admitting that things might go wrong but making it clear that it is your company's policy to make them right goes a lot further than claiming that nothing ever goes wrong. If it turns into a he-said/she-said between you and your client's source, who do you think will win that disagreement?

Remember, there are some shady companies or industries out there that do give customers reason for concern. Consider a company's reputation before you sign on as a salesperson so you can avoid having this objection carry any water.

# Objection 14

"I've never heard of your company."

## What They're Really Saying

"How can I trust that you'll deliver what you've proposed if you have no track record? What if you're just out to make a quick buck?"

This is a fair concern that you will likely come up against if you're with a newer business or an unusual industry. If you're conducting business over the phone, it can be all the more difficult.

Most new companies are well aware that this is an issue for their sales force. They should provide you with all kinds of data and materials proving the solvency and good standing of your company.

## How to Respond

More than a response, what you need is a database of willing references. Have a few people on hand who can vouch for your services. Your company may provide some testimonials for your marketing materials, but it's even better if you can create your own. Working with your own testimonials will leave you with people who are just a phone call away if need be.

This isn't really the direct route of response, so here's an example of its implementation.

> "I understand where you're coming from. I've had a few of my past clients voice the same concern. Our company has been around for five years now, and we've done millions of dollars in business. While that's obviously a great thing, I also keep a list of personal references and testimonials from local clients I've done business with, just in case someone has the same concern as you."

You don't want your past clients to be bombarded, nor do you want to give out their personal information, so it might be best to start with the testimonials. Let your new client know that he can get in touch with any of the people you've listed if you get their approval.

# Objection 15

"I found a better price."

## What They're Really Saying

> "I found a better price, but I'm still talking to you because there is room to make the sale."

Unless you have a very courteous client, you're not likely to get a call from her telling you that she's going with another client because of a better price. Most will avoid you and then simply tell you no once you catch up to them.

If the client is offering up that she has found a better price but has not made a decision, she might be digging for a price match. If you can do it, do it! The customer thought highly enough of you to give you the opportunity to retain her business. However, because price-matching isn't usually the way businesses work, you may have to go another route.

## How to Respond

If your client didn't voice price as being the most important part of the transaction from the beginning, it's not likely that it's a pure pricing situation. Remind the customer of the needs you're filling to keep her on track.

Obviously, your competition is attempting to fill the same needs. This is when you need to go head to head with the enemy. Remember, don't talk down about the competition. Simply point out the advantages of doing business with your firm as opposed to the guys across town. You have to fight price with features and benefits.

# Objection 16

"I found better quality elsewhere."

## What They're Really Saying

"Someone else is doing what you're doing, only better."

It's important that you get as much information from your client as possible about your competition's offerings. For you or your customer to make a comparison, it must be apples to apples.

This is a tough objection to deal with, because perception of quality is in the eye of the beholder. You may know you have a better product, but something about your competition sits better with the consumer.

You may also have a product that isn't quite as good as the competition. This is when you want to avoid the apples-to-apples comparison and shoot for apples to oranges. If your competition has you flat-out beat on one aspect, focus on the ones where you excel. Use the features that your competition doesn't have.

## How to Respond

"What did you like better about the competition?"

Have an open conversation. This question will help you determine whether you should go head to head with the competition or whether you should focus on a different aspect of your business.

"I know A+ Food Distributors has higher-graded meats, but ours all come from local farmers."

In this example, the sales rep went head-on to the concern over the quality of meats. This may or may not matter to the client, but it is a great feature to point out in a direct comparison.

"I know A+ Food Distributors has higher-graded meats, but we guarantee daily delivery. A+ does deliveries only twice per week."

In this example, the sales rep indirectly conceded to the meat quality but brought the focus to a place where his company can't be beat.

When all else fails, fight quality objections with price (assuming your price is lower).

> "I know A+ has some of the best meats available, but they're going to charge you $2.59 per pound of ground beef while we have it priced at $1.89."

Even though the customer led in with a quality objection, there's nothing wrong with reminding him of the bottom line.

# Objection 17

"Why is it so cheap?"

## What They're Really Saying

> "What's the catch? Either this is going to be an unacceptable product or you're going to stick me for more money later."

Don't hold your breath for this one. It rarely happens, even if you're the cheapest firm in town. However, people are becoming more and more cautious with the rising amount of fraud and number of fly-by-night businesses.

Make sure your pricing is transparent. If it's cheap because you're not telling the customer about future costs or charges, you're scamming the consumer. If the price is absurdly low but there's a legitimate reason, share it with your customer to put her at ease.

## How to Respond

> "People find our televisions to be far cheaper than the competition's. Although everything we sell is new, it's always last year's models. We get extras on a discount and pass the savings on to you."

Again, this is not a frequent objection; just be certain to meet it with honesty and transparency.

# Objection 18

"Can I try it for free?"

## What They're Really Saying

"I don't want to commit to anything I'm not totally sold on."

Depending on your industry, your competition might be letting people test out their product to get them hooked. If your company allows for it, go ahead and let the customer have at it! If there is no way to try your product or get it risk/return free, you'll have to do the convincing yourself.

## How to Respond

"Unfortunately, we aren't able to let our clients try out our products. However, I have many personal testimonials from past clients that I can share with you."

Your trusty testimonial sheet comes in handy once again. The customer knows you can tell him how great your product is until you're blue in the face. Hearing it from someone else can help give him the confidence to make a buying decision.

Sales positions exist because people need to be convinced to make certain types of purchases. If you can't do it on your own and you don't have the ability to sample, a third-party endorsement is the best way to secure uncertain business.

# Objection 19

"No solicitations!"

## What They're Really Saying

"We don't want to spend all of our time talking to hundreds of salespeople. When we need something, we'll go get it."

These customers are usually business owners. Everyone and their mother wants to get in with the buyer or owner and sell her anything they can. After a time, business owners may become frustrated and simply deny any new salespeople.

As dire as the situation might seem, these business owners still need products or services. You must be very careful and low pressure with these types of clients, as they will take time to nurture.

Trust me from experience; sales calls that start with this objection can sometimes turn into your best clients. Most salespeople will either immediately fold or become way too pushy and confrontational. Anyone who finesses her way into a relationship with these kinds of clients is rewarded with longstanding loyalty.

## How to Respond

"I'm sorry to bother you. I'm new to this position and just wanted to get out and meet some new people."

Most sales managers and trainers will tell you never to say you're sorry and to act like an equal with a right to conduct business. In general, this is a great idea, but when you solicit someone who doesn't want to be solicited, you have to back down and show some humility.

Mentioning that you're new helps to build relationships with clients who do not want to be solicited. They know/think they can mold you and don't expect an expert salesperson to be bothering them for business at all times.

Send an apology letter. Yes, most of you are disagreeing right now, and any sales managers still reading this book are likely going to put it down. Trust me; type a letter, hand-sign it, and send it off with your business card. Keep it extremely short.

Dear Mrs. Livingston,

I apologize for catching you at a bad time the other day. I'm sure you're busy as can be, and talking to a new newspaper advertising sales rep was dead last on your list. If you'd ever like to talk about advertising in the local paper, I've included my contact information.

Sincerely,

Mary Martin

Trust me—I've never met another sales rep who deals with this objection in this way. A letter like this is so eyebrow-raising that you're bound to get several callbacks.

There are many ways to overcome objections, but the best way is to avoid them all together by completing a need-based sales process.

# Action Plan

✓ Determine the common objections you come up against.

✓ Decide who you can consult about creative ways to overcome these objections.

✓ Make a comprehensive list of testimonials to build trust with your new clientele.

✓ Practice overcoming objections with other salespeople.

# Chapter 7

# Goal Setting

- Sales Goals
- Short-Term Goals
- Activity Goals
- Personal Goals
- Daily Plans
- Action Plan

I have been spoiled by sales.

Think about every other position in the workforce that isn't sales related. People spend all year trying to do a good job, trying to make their bosses happy, hoping and praying for a promotion or raise. They work and work and then sit down for an evaluation at the end of the year.

> "You've done a great job this year! However, with the poor economy, there isn't any room for a big pay raise. Also, we're not doing any promoting because most people are staying put for job security. Thanks for your hard work, and we'll go over this again next year."

How can anyone be motivated by that? How can anyone expect to achieve higher income based on difficult-to-track results and personal relationships?

Sales and self-employment (which always requires some level of sales) are the only fields where you can truly control your income. It's a very cut-and-dried system, tracked and built around reaching goals.

## Sales Goals

The next time you sit down in a sales meeting to discuss goals, think about what we just discussed. Think about all the people who have very little control over their income. Company-imposed sales goals are not set up to micromanage you or to stress you out of your mind, they're built to get you on track to the income you desire.

*Sales goals are designed for you to make a profit for both you and the company.*

These goals exist for your employer to track your production. They are experts at configuring goals that will make you profitable to them while also making money for you. The numbers are based on a variety of factors, such as past performance of the individual salesperson and the overall activity of the sales force. It might sometimes feel as if they just pick high numbers out of the blue, but a lot goes into the process.

## Compensation

Early in your career, it's important to become familiar with your pay structure. Base salary, commissions, and bonuses all play into the particular goal formula your company subscribes to. Take a look at how any of those can change based on performance. Find out whether your commission changes when you exceed goals or if anything is held back when you fall short.

When you have every piece of the puzzle, put it together. Figure out what you'll make if you hit every goal on the nose. It should be a reasonable amount and a familiar number shared in the interview stages. If the number is too high or too low, you'll need to get clarification from management as soon as possible. Most of you will not run into this problem, but I have seen some variation on this in the past.

> Meeting your goals should yield you a reasonable income for the year. If the number seems too high or too low, talk to your manager to clarify the company's goals and compensation system.

If meeting your goals results in a low income for the year, there may be a few things in play. Best-case scenario, your goals are only minimum goals. These are numbers you must hit to keep your job. Anything above and beyond is icing on the cake and money in your pocket. Some sales positions that pay straight commission and treat you like a contractor operate with these lower numbers.

There is also a miniscule chance that the company pays badly and turns over salespeople on a regular basis. If you work in a call center or a retail shop with a high volume of work, and hitting your goals still keeps you in the $20,000 range, don't expect to make $40,000 the next year. For some people, this may be a comfortable income level, and they might like the security of attainable goals in a call center or retail atmosphere, but a position like this is not going to result in major income until you move into management.

The biggest concern with goals netting a low income is found when you've been promised the potential for a high income. Do the math. How much higher over your goals must you reach to make the kind of money you want? Is that kind of volume sustainable?

If meeting your goals results in a high income for the year, there are some other things to consider. First and foremost, you may be in a high-end sales position. That being said, I'm not sure whether a lot of arms dealers or national advertising agents are reading this book.…

Unusually high income tied to hitting your regular goals is typically a red flag. Management may have decided to take an overly eager approach to motivating their sales force and set the bar a little bit too high. This might not sound like the words of a true salesperson, but every person selling insurance, cars, or cell phones cannot likely be on track to make a six-figure income. It's certainly possible, but it should not be the standard for an entire sales force.

These lofty numbers can also be used in the recruiting process. If people see that hitting your goals makes you $100,000, they assume that enough people are doing it for the goals to be set so high in the first place.

If your company has goals that you are certain would be a stretch for you to reach, have a conversation with your manager. Are you going to keep your job if you only reach 50 percent of your goal? Will your income be severely impacted if you don't hit such a high threshold? Considering that the company may be using these numbers to lure and motivate, it's still possible that you will be able to work and make an income without ever having to reach these unrealistic goals.

Use your common sense and do your research. Know your industry's standard for income and stay on top of these numbers.

## Meetings

With sales goals come sales meetings. With sales meetings come a variety of emotions and discussions. Anyone who has spent time in sales is familiar with the feeling. Sometimes, you can't wait to share numbers with your peers. Maybe you shattered the numbers for the week, month, or year, and all you want to do is stand on the table while people cheer you on as if you just scored the winning touchdown in the Super Bowl. Of course, you'll end up playing it cool as if it's business as usual while everyone congratulates you with a twinge of jealousy. Your manager will look at you with a smile and a nod and then move on to the next person's numbers.

Then the next week rolls around. You spent two days dealing with car trouble and another three days chasing down clients who wouldn't return your calls. This time, you're sitting in your seat and cringing on the inside but trying to keep it cool on the outside. It's almost time for you to announce your big fat goose egg for the week. You flip through some excuses in your head, but no matter what you do, the manager who was grinning at you last week is wondering this week why you were even hired. Your peers barely make eye contact, and you can't wait to get out of the meeting.

Everyone has felt some piece of those two extremes. You get to feel the emotional and financial roller coaster that is sales in each and every sales meeting. This design is not in error. Salespeople are driven by income, but humans are also driven by accolades and disappointment.

Even the man or woman making six figures feels uncomfortable about turning in a bad week or month. Across the table, the person who you've assumed is starving from lack of income can be on top of the world with just one good sales meeting.

Recognizing that these meetings are meant to motivate you is the first step in getting the most out of them. Feed off the positive energy and allow yourself to get competitive. Money in your pocket feels great, but so does a pat on the back.

> Sales meetings are designed to motivate you and keep you on track—regardless of whether you had a good week or a bad one.

Obviously, these meetings aren't just about building warm fuzzies or kicking you while you're down. They're also intended to keep you on track. Some people tend to procrastinate. Maybe your goal for the year is to sell 150 units of product. Procrastinators might have 40 units sold toward the end of the year and then try to scramble to sell 110 more in the last few months. These meetings keep you in check and play a huge role in setting smaller, more manageable goals. These same procrastinators would be in better shape if they aimed to sell three units per week. Meetings help you manage your short-term goals to make your long-term achievements.

## Short-Term Goals

Different industries with different sales cycles break down and monitor sales with a wide range of goals. Some are yearly, quarterly, monthly, weekly, and even daily. The important thing to remember is that your smaller goals help you reach the larger long-term ones. If you meet your daily goals, you'll meet your weekly goals; if you meet your weekly goals, you meet your monthlies; and so on.

> Short-term goals will help you reach long-term ones.

For guaranteed success in sales, there are no benchmarks more important than your short-term goals. You might get an email telling you your pace for the quarter. There may be a dry-erase board tracking your progress toward a successful year. With every tracking method available, your focus must be on the shortest reasonable term.

Some sales processes simply cannot be tracked on a daily basis. Advertising sales of all kinds typically cannot be tracked on anything less than a week-by-week level. However, most types of retail or low-ticket consumer goods can be tracked daily.

## Tracking Short-Term Goals

*If your company doesn't provide goal-tracking tools, put together your own plan.*

Many companies will provide more than enough tools to track your progress in sales. It's important that you take advantage of this help and not look at it as a burden. If there is no short-term goal setting in place, put together your own plan.

First, figure out what your yearly goal is. Read closely: figure out what *your* yearly goal is. It's not always the one dictated to you by management. You do have to play by their rules, but assuming you want to exceed their expectations, you must take action on your own.

Next, figure out what the shortest reasonable duration of time is for tracking. The easiest rule of thumb is that your goal has to be at least one sale or a set dollar value. Is it possible to get one sale per day? Per week? Biweekly? How long does it take you to sell $5,000 of your service? What about $800 of your product? The numbers may vary, but use your best judgment to figure out what would be most manageable.

### Example 1

Tiffany works in advertising sales. She makes 15 percent straight commission on all of her sales. Her company targets her to make $45,000. This means she would have to sell $300,000 in annual advertising. But Tiffany is a go-getter. She wants to make at least $60,000. To do so, she'll need to sell $400,000 in annual advertising.

Because Tiffany is able to make two or three sales per week with varying dollar values, she decides to break down her goals on a week-to-week basis.

Assuming Tiffany takes two weeks of vacation, she has 50 work-weeks to meet her yearly goal. Do the simple math: $400,000 divided by 50 weeks means Tiffany will have to sell $8,000 of advertising per week. Because she doesn't have at least one sale per day, it wouldn't make much sense for her to break it down any further.

## Example 2

Andre works in a credit card company's call center. He has a base salary of $25,000. For every customer that he gets to increase his or her credit limit or to do a balance transfer, he gets a $10 bonus.

Andre's company already tracks on a daily basis. If his coworkers hit their goals of two bonuses per day, they make $30,000 (2 bonuses times $10 times 250 work days + $25,000 base salary).

Andre wants to exceed these goals and shoots for four bonuses per day. This will land him at $35,000 per year. Instead of even leaving it to daily tracking, Andre assumes correctly that he needs to make one transaction every two hours. With the high pace and volume of calls he gets each day, he feels it's an achievable goal, even if it's broken down to the hourly level.

## Example 3

Michele works as a real estate agent. As a self-employed agent, she earns straight commission. Her brokerage will keep her on board as long as she makes the minimum to pay her desk, technology, and licensing fees.

Michele wants to make more than $100,000 this year. She knows that half of her income will have to go toward paying her bills as an entrepreneur. Advertising, signs, business supplies, fees, and an assistant all have their price.

With a target of $200,000 into her business, she sets out with a calculator to figure her yearly goals. After her agency gets its cut, she makes 2.5 percent for every house she sells or helps a new owner purchase.

The average home price in her area is $200,000, so she stands to make $5,000 per transaction. This means Michele must be involved in 40 real estate transactions per year as a buyer's or seller's agent.

This number obviously cannot be tracked on a weekly basis, so she self imposes a short-term goal of 3.3 transactions per month. Some houses will go for more or less than others, and some months have more activity than most, but this is the most efficient way for her to track her progress.

This final example leads us on to the next type of goal setting. Although Michele's job as a real estate agent is generally considered a sales position, it's not an industry where you can go out and "sell" someone into a house. The house has to be priced appropriately and fit the needs of what the buyers are looking for. If she's not out there selling, but she's doing a great job at facilitating, what can she do to increase her chances of hitting these transaction goals?

# Activity Goals

*Activity goals ensure that you take the action required to realize your sales goals.*

Someone like Michele would benefit most by setting activity goals. Sales goals are great, but activity goals make sure you're taking the necessary action to make these sales happen. Activity goals keep you on top of your prospecting while making sure you are servicing your existing customer base.

Sales goals are very easy to set: I need to get $X$ in sales to earn $Y$ per year. Activity goals take more time and careful consideration to craft to your personal abilities.

## Mandated Activity

Most sales positions will mandate or at least suggest some level of activity. This might seem like micromanaging because…well, it is! But don't feel as if this is just your managers trying to watch every step you take. Certain levels of activity yield results even for some of the least capable salespeople.

What management doesn't consider when building these activity goals is the individual ability of the sales rep. They use a law of averages (and then add some) to calculate what they feel is the best way to spend your time.

## Phone Tracking

One of the most basic ways activity is tracked is by the number of calls a salesperson makes. Some companies simply track the number; others will chart your minute-by-minute phone time. Some sales forces also count calls, but only the ones lasting for a certain duration.

There's no debating the value in this activity. The more time you spend making calls, the more contacts, meetings, and sales you will have.

There are only two things you need to remember about the phone-call goals your management sets for you. First, don't make the calls just to go through the motions. This doesn't help anyone, and the obvious purpose is to turn these calls into business. Second, make sure you meet these goals. I've seen a lot of people fall short of their goals but try to qualify it by talking up the value of the calls made. You may be right, and you could have conducted higher-quality calls that yield results, but why not meet your goal and make even more? If you combine actual effort with your activity goals and hit the number management is asking for, there is almost no way for you to miss your overall sales goals. For the few sales managers who haven't felt alienated by this book thus far and have made it to this section, you're welcome.

For management, getting people on the phones is like pulling teeth. It takes time for people to feel comfortable picking up the phone to set appointments or sell, but management is only pressing you to do so because it works.

## Tracking Sales Appointments

Tracking actual sales appointments is yet another way to make sure you're going about the most important activity, selling.

You could make hundreds of calls per day, but that means nothing if you don't set a face-to-face appointment or move into the sales process over the phone. Getting in front of people is where all the real sales action happens. By monitoring your sales-appointment numbers, you and your managers can work on your sales process if you aren't closing a high enough percentage through these meetings.

A heavy volume of sales calls doesn't mean anything if you aren't following up those calls with sales appointments.

It's very important that you provide honest numbers when tracking sales appointments. Phone calls are easy to track because most companies subscribe to a service that allows them to track your individual activity. Sales meetings are different.

There is a temptation to call every visit, handshake, or coffee a full-blown sales appointment. You want to have activity to report in your meetings if your management openly tracks these numbers. You want to look busy and show that you're out there trying to make a sale. Unfortunately, inflating these numbers has the opposite effect.

When you have a high number of sales appointments set against a low number of closes, it looks like you're out there in front of potential clients fumbling and bumbling your way out of a sale. If anything, you should err on the side of under-tracking.

"Well, we talked a little about product, but this was more of a getting-to-know-you meeting."

Fine, don't count it. Even if you're closing the same amount of business as others, a poor ratio will garner some attention from your managers.

The rep with six sales appointments and three closes for the week likely will be left alone and even praised. The other one with 20 sales appointments and three closes has clearly accomplished something, but it seems he or she may need help with the sales process.

The best way to avoid these ratio issues is to break down tracking sales appointments by their purpose. Track introduction meetings. Track presentations. Track closing attempts. If you keep these separate yourself or via your managers, you will have a better grasp of how you are performing.

## Other Trackables

While phone calls and sales meetings are the easiest and most obvious goals to track, there are other trackables that you or your management might consider.

As stated earlier, breaking down the purpose of sales meetings or even calls can have some benefit. Some days you might make 40 calls and have no sales or appointments because all of your activity was related to servicing existing clients or doing follow-up.

Emails and correspondences are rarely tracked, yet they do provide good information about your activity levels. Follow-up mailings are an important part of the sales process. Also, keeping track of these numbers makes it easier for you to know who you have been reaching out to and who needs to hear a live voice or see your face.

This might go without saying, especially if you have a base salary, but keeping track of your hours and days worked should also play a part in your activity tracking. Your week might look bad because you missed a day from illness or personal issues. Maybe your week looks great, but you realize that it took you 65 hours to accomplish this. Tracking time is especially important for people who are not mandated to do so through their company. You may enjoy the freedom of not having a set schedule, but if you don't hold yourself accountable to time, you're not going to make any money.

*Tracking your time will help you quantify your numbers.*

You should track maintenance time and calls in a very separate fashion. Maintaining existing relationships is important, but not at the cost of losing new potential clients. You must find a very healthy balance based on where you are in your career. Newer reps should spend most of their time finding and working with new clients. Some veteran reps may spend virtually all of their time working with established clientele.

Track your spending, too. Salespeople are always on the go. They burn more gas, eat out more, treat people to meals, travel, and so on. Tracking your spending on a business as well as a personal level is so important that I have included a later chapter discussing the lifestyle and finances of a successful sales professional.

## Personalized Activity

This is where the math gets tricky, but the real value can be found in setting activity goals.

Using the data you've gathered over time, you can use the numbers to figure out what kind of activity you need to meet your sales goals. You will find in time that a certain number of calls nets you a certain number of appointments, which nets you a certain number of sales.

Customizing this information will be extremely helpful to you and will also help you find your strengths and weaknesses, depending on how much you are tracking.

Consider this example. Dennis wants to figure out how many calls he needs to make to reach his weekly goal of two sales. In his first month, Dennis made 500 calls that netted him 25 appointments and five sales. Working backwards, the math is simple: Dennis made five sales in 25 meetings. That's five meetings for one sale.

Dennis made 25 appointments from making 500 calls. That's one meeting for every 20 calls made. If Dennis needs five meetings for a sale, and he gets one meeting per 20 calls, he'll have to make 100 calls per week to make a sale.

Of course, these numbers are round, and there's nothing saying his conversion rate can't change, but this activity-driven goal will net him the sales results he's looking for. When he gets better on the phones, he might get an appointment every 15 calls. Maybe he'll do a better job of uncovering needs and close one out of three sales. Tracking these numbers closely will help him through his entire sales career.

## Personal Goals

Don't neglect your personal goals in the interest of your business goals. You need a balance of both.

With all this talk of business goals, it's important to remember to have personal goals as well. The whole purpose of an income is to drive the things you want out of life.

Now that you have your activity and income goals in place, what personal goals do you want to accomplish through your income and lifestyle? Goals to save money are the most obvious. Other goals are of a personal level and hold just as much importance as any number of phone calls or sales meetings you've been tracking. Treat these goals in the same way as you would business ones. Break them down into small, manageable chunks.

Here are some ideas for personal goals that can be driven by meeting your goals as a salesperson:

> "Each year, I want to put $6,000 into my retirement. This means I will have to contribute $250 from each of my biweekly pay periods."

> "I want to make a down payment of $20,000 on a house next year. I'm going to increase my call activity this year and spend an extra five hours each week prospecting."

I personally love the previous example. Someone who has broken down his sales success and earnings far enough could know that five hours of extra time per week would net that income.

> "I want to go to Europe for the entire month of September. I'm going to surpass my sales goals for the year by then to pay for the added costs of travel and the month of missing income."

Sure, this person would have to be straight commissioned or a business owner, but the only way to reach a goal is to define it and set it into motion.

# Daily Plans

To reach any of your goals—whether personal or business, short term or long term—you must build your day to facilitate your sales and activities.

If you know you need to make 50 calls in a day and hold two appointments while doing two hours of paperwork, block your time so that you can do so. Convert your goals into daily steps so that you have a plan to achieve them.

Without a daily plan, you run the risk of not hitting your short-term or activity goals. You might get carried away on a project and realize that you spent six hours gathering data on a large new client. Are you going to stay the extra time, or are you going to put the calls off to the next day?

# Action Plan

Goals of all kinds will put you on target for the personal and professional life you desire. Keep these key things in mind as you start to construct your goals.

✓ Know every way and rate in which you are compensated.

✓ Know how you can tie your compensation to your goals.

✓ Be aware of the goals mandated by your company.

✓ Determine what goals you are going to set for yourself.

✓ Determine what short-term goals you will set for yourself to reach your long-term goals.

✓ Determine how much activity it takes for you to make your sale.

✓ Decide how much you will track.

✓ Think about any areas for concern in your sales career that could benefit from tracking and goal setting.

✓ Determine your personal goals.

# Chapter 8

# Continual Prospecting Techniques

- Referrals
- Asking for the Referral
- Soliciting Referrals
- Referral Troubleshooting
- Prospecting Your Existing Database
- Becoming an Expert
- Action Plan

In the earlier chapter on prospecting, we focused on the basics. It's important to learn the basics of how to reach out to new clients, but to have long-term success, prospecting must be a continuous process. You're not always going to have leads to call on and hundreds of calls to make if you don't continuously refill the pipeline of potential clientele.

# Referrals

The most effective way of keeping yourself busy as a salesperson is through referrals. You'll notice that we didn't discuss referrals in the earlier chapter. You might also notice that your brand-new sales manager in your brand-new sales position is breathing down your neck for more referral-based work.

*Timing is key when asking for referrals.*

The reality of the sales prospecting business is that you cannot dive headfirst into the world of referrals. You must have serviced your clients to ask for referral business. Sales managers may tell you otherwise—grab at as many new leads as you can, no matter how untimely your actions must be. Sure, you may garner a few leads with these overbearing tactics, but it's important to have some real purpose to the referrals you're asking for. You can see the importance of timing with these two quick comparisons.

Consider a client you have just met for an initial meeting. You haven't even asked for his business yet, but under the pressure of management, you begin to ask for referrals. How can someone give you a true referral if you've never serviced him before? Asking too soon implies that you're going to churn and burn your clients as quickly as possible.

Now consider a client you've been working with for several weeks. You've made the sale, and your product or service has been implemented. You check in with the client to find that she is happy with her experience. This is the prime time to ask for a referral. The client will refer you to people in her life because she has given you her stamp of approval.

This stamp of approval is what makes the referral so valuable in the first place. You're given access to a person you may not have had the chance to solicit otherwise. The simple contact information is worth quite a bit to you. However, your ability to make a familiar connection with someone the prospect knows that you've satisfied is what makes referrals the number-one way to find new business.

There are two basic steps to the referral process: asking for the referral and contacting the warm lead.

# Asking for the Referral

As stated earlier, there are very specific times when you should be on the lookout for a referral. Depending on the length of your sales process, this may be upon immediate delivery of your product or a short time after your service has been initiated. The client must have a full picture of how you are filling her needs before she can comfortably pass you on to her friends, family, and associates.

As a good sales rep, you should be following up with your client after the sale, regardless of your intention to ask for referrals. It's important to make sure the client got what she was looking for, and it also shows that you're serious about doing continued business if your industry allows for this.

After confirming that your client is happy up to this point in the process, there are several ways you can launch into the referral process. There are no tricks to getting more leads; just find something that makes you feel comfortable so that you'll ask for referrals each and every time. If the verbiage feels forced, you won't want to take this step to begin with.

Find a way that you feel comfortable with to ask for referrals.

The following sections provide some examples of how to ask for referrals.

## Example 1

"I'm glad to hear you're so happy with our service! As you know, a big part of my job is finding other people like you who I can help with our services. Is there anyone you can think of that I should consider calling?"

This first example is a very generic and straightforward approach. You've confirmed that the customer is happy, you've explained why you're going to ask, and then you've proceeded with your inquiry. When you get comfortable with this more generic approach, there are many other ways to lay the groundwork.

### Example 2

"Tim, it has been a pleasure working with you. To be honest, you're the ideal client for someone in my position. Knowing that like people tend to associate with each other, do you know anyone else I should be contacting?"

This example is perfect for someone who seems to enjoy having his ego stroked. A business owner or professional who has worked hard to get where he is might respond well to this approach. Anyone else with an abundant sense of pride would work as well. In this example, you've made the client feel good, like your primary target, and rightfully assumed that he associates with people of the same caliber. This kind of approach can be extremely useful for people who are soliciting a very specific type of client, in the way pharmaceutical reps work exclusively with doctors, for example.

### Example 3

"Lauren, I'm glad we were able to provide the right solutions to meet your needs. A large part of my business is meeting other professionals like you to build my circle of influence. Do you have anyone in your circle of influence that you would like to introduce me to?"

This example is similar to the previous ones in that you've made it clear that the sales process came to an amiable completion. The "circle of influence" comment might seem a bit canned, but it makes your client focus on people over whom she feels she has persuasive power. You take the step even further by asking for the referral as an introduction. This implies that your client will play a hand in helping you make the connection. Maybe Lauren will place a call for you or even meet you and the lead for coffee and a quick introduction. Turning a referral into a full-blown personal introduction starts you out way ahead of the game with your new client.

### Example 4

"I'm glad you're satisfied with our services, and I look forward to working with you again in the future! Before I go, is there anyone else in your area who might be worth calling on or who you could put me in contact with? I really like this neighborhood, and we'd love to do more business out here."

This angle can be very specific to contractors or anyone else working on a residential basis. First, you've locked in a future business opportunity. Second, you're asking for a specific type of lead. You want more people in this neighborhood or area for which your client likely has an affinity. You've given him credit for where he lives and banked on the fact that he likely knows his neighbors.

## Example 5

"John, I'm glad you're happy with our product! You know, lately this product has been extremely popular with college students as well. Can you think of anyone in college who might be worth calling on in the near future?"

This example could be taken a variety of ways, but the core idea remains intact. Asking your client for a very specific demographic forces him to think about specific people. Depending on your product or service, you should already know some of your most popular types of clientele. Do you know any college students? Do you know any newlyweds? Retirees? Motorcycle owners? Any question that gets your client thinking about specific people in his life will help you narrow his search. This is a great way to replace the generic, "Do you know anyone who might need our services?" approach. *You* know what people tend to need your service. Your client can help you find them with a bit of direction.

Not all referrals need to be secured immediately after the sale. You might get some, or the client might not have anyone to give you at the time. This is why you must do some of your referral farming even further down the road. This holds especially true for salespeople who work with infrequent buyers, such as real estate agents, roofers, large-machinery salespeople, investment salespeople, and so on.

## Example 6

"Jarred, it's Mark from XYZ Realty. How's the new house treating you? [Make some small talk about the purchase and product here.] Well, it was good catching up with you. Listen, do you know of anyone else looking to buy or sell a house in the near future? Just trying to reach out to as many people as I can during this busy season."

Mark might have sold this house to Jarred six months ago. Although he asked for referrals after the closing, this is a simple follow-up call to check on his client and to look for more leads. Maybe Jarred had no one to refer last time, but just a few weeks ago his pregnant sister-in-law was talking about moving into a bigger home.

### Example 7

"Kim, it's Jeff from ZYX Roofing! How are you? I'm just calling because we like to follow up after a year or so to make sure the roof is living up to your standards. It is? Great! Hey, we're getting ready for the new season, and I was wondering whether you knew of anyone in your neighborhood getting quotes right now or looking for a roof."

This is a great example that gives an obvious primary purpose to the call. Jeff is following up to check on the roof. However, the secondary question adds value to this otherwise customer-service call.

Asking for referrals at a later date helps you beyond simply acquiring new clientele. It's good customer service, and it keeps you in the front of your clients' minds for their future buying needs.

## Soliciting Referrals

You've gotten several warm leads from your past clients, but now it's time to do something with them! Depending on how you have set up the lead to begin with, you may go after this new client in several different ways.

You might end up with just a name and phone number. There's nothing wrong with this, and it's likely how eight out of ten of your referrals will begin. The following sections provide some examples of how to open up with your new potential clients.

### Example 1

"Hi Darcy, this is Matt from ABC Financial. Your friend, Mike Brown, is a client of mine, and he suggested I give you a call."

Although this is clearly the lead-off generic example, there is a unique style found in its simplicity. Matt doesn't give any purpose or direction for the call other than the fact that he works with her friend, Mike Brown, and he was directed to give her a call. This approach leaves the ball in her court and lets her feel comfortable directing the conversation. She might follow up with, "Great! I was looking to talk with an investment advisor." But more likely than not, it will be a bit more difficult than that.

"Mike Brown told you to call me? Why?"

"Well, I handle his investments, and your name came up when I asked him whether he knew of other like-minded people who might be in need of investment services."

You can see how the simple opening will lead to a variety of responses and at least get you talking to this lead.

## Example 2

"Hi, is this Travis Johnson's friend, Jerry? Oh, it is—good. My name is Wendy, and I do Travis's bookkeeping. He said you might be looking for similar services, so I thought I'd give you a call."

This is a really informal way of accessing the lead. Wendy simply confirms the connection at the beginning with a question that will leave Jerry thinking on a familiar and friendly level. She even goes on to make it clear that Travis was the one who suggested that the connection be made.

## Example 3

"Hi, Anna. My name is Burt, and I handle all of your Uncle Roger's insurance needs. He said that you're in the process of buying a home and might need some assistance in getting homeowner's insurance."

Although this is a bit more formal than the previous example, Burt is making a very purposeful call. He found out through an active referral conversation with Roger that his niece is buying a home. This ultimately works twice as well, because there is a family connection, and a need has already made itself evident.

## Example 4

"Hi Shirley, this is Eric from AAA Auto Sales. Your friend, Tim Marshall, gave me your number, but I'm not entirely sure why."

This is a bit of a risky way to work a referral, but it can start you off on a much faster pace uncovering your new client's needs. Although you run the risk of sounding uninformed, you're really getting your lead to come up with her own needs without even asking.

"Oh, that is strange. You know, I've had my car for almost 10 years now. Maybe he was trying to give me a hint!"

Whatever it might be, Shirley is looking for the need to qualify her friend giving up her number.

In the perfect referral world, your current client will make the introduction in one way or another. First, he might make the call to the lead on your behalf.

"Hey, Sam, it's Rick. I know you were thinking about getting a pool installed, so I thought I'd give you my guy's number. His name is Dave Richardson, and he was extremely helpful throughout the whole process."

This is a great way to start a new working relationship, but there is one thing you *must* do for this to be successful—follow up with your previous customer. Chances are slim that the new lead will pick up the phone and call you on his own. Talk to your original customer to find out how the conversation went and then ask to place a call yourself. This should be twice as easy as calling an already warmed referral. For example:

"Hi, Sam. This is Dave Richardson from Premier Pools. I think you talked to a friend of mine, Rick Jacobs, about getting a pool installed?"

Not only does Dave have the opportunity to reference a person for this referral, he can also throw a prior conversation into the mix. Added points for referring to Rick as a friend as opposed to a client.

# Referral Troubleshooting

Finding and using referrals can sometimes be met with mixed reactions and expectations. Understand that many people may not be comfortable giving you their friends' and family members' names, even if you've done your job flawlessly. No one wants to sic a salesperson on someone she cares about.

There are a few ways to remedy this objection. The first way might actually leave you in a better position than if they had given you a name and number when prompted.

> "You know, I completely understand where you're coming from. Let's do this. Think of a few friends you know who might need my service. Give them a call and ask them whether they'd be interested in talking to me. This way, they won't feel as if you threw them to the wolves, but I'll still have an opportunity to provide them with great service."

Now you've got your own client working for you, and he doesn't have to feel like he has wronged his friend or family member. This process might take a bit longer than you calling on your own, but your new lead will be twice as warmed.

Second, you can simply tell the client you will not use her name. If there is enough trust in your working relationship, this should help her get over the fear of referral. *Stick to your word!* There's nothing worse than alienating a good client by throwing her name out when she specifically asked you not to. Just treat the lead like you would treat one from your own lead-generation process.

Finally, you have the option to walk away without a lead. Some people simply will not ask for leads. But keep servicing this customer well, and there's a good chance he'll come around if he remains happy down the road.

Remember, taking good care of your customers in the first place will eventually lead to some totally unsolicited referrals. Someone might call in and ask to meet with you because your name came up among friends or family.

Taking good care of your clients can sometimes lead to unsolicited referrals.

# Prospecting Your Existing Database

Not all new business has to come from new clients. Part of the referral process is calling old clients to ask for new people to contact. Depending on your industry, you might even have the opportunity to solicit your past clients for more business.

## Record Keeping

To do continual business with your existing clientele, it's important to keep good records of all your business transactions and meetings. Keeping a digital or hard copy file depicting all of the transactions, notes, calls, and so on that you've had with your client will help you scour for business at a later time.

During some sales meetings, you will uncover needs that you might not have to address immediately. You might sell your client another product, but it is crucial that you take note of her developing needs. A boat salesperson might sell someone a ski boat when he has a family with children, but maybe that customer mentioned buying a yacht when his youngest goes off to college five years down the road. Notes about these types of comments can yield great successes in the long run.

Paying attention to the buying habits of your clientele can help you position new products or services based on their account history. A machinery salesperson might be focused on selling large earth-moving machines. Down the road, a new type of forklift might become available. By taking good notes and paying attention to client history, this salesperson could get back in touch with a warehouse manager he hasn't spoken to in some time. Although most of his focus has been on bulldozers and trucks, he will be able to quickly go back to his limited database of forklift users without doing a lot of digging.

## Soliciting Past Clients

You've decided that you have a new product or service that would be worth the attention of your past clients. What is the best way to reach out to them once again?

First, make sure you continuously stay in touch with your existing database so that this re-solicitation goes smoothly. Send holiday cards or emails and be sure to call your past clients from time to time, depending on your industry. Now, instead of saying, "Hey, remember me from six years ago?" it can be another, "Hey, how are you doing?" type of call.

Staying in touch with past clients makes it easier to re-solicit them later.

Next, use the comfort level of your relationship to set up your sales meeting. These leads are warmed beyond hot simply because you've done business in the past. Don't throw all levels of formality out the window, but speak to the level of your existing relationship. For example:

> "Virginia, it's Kayla from ABC Supply. How are you? We're about to roll out some new product, and I had a couple of ideas I wanted you to take a look at. Do you have time for some coffee or to come into the office?"

This is a very comfortable and assumptive opening with a client Kayla already knows. If their relationship is strong enough, Virginia likely will come in or have a coffee because of the trust factor built over the years.

Once the appointment is set, it's important to *stop* relying on the existing relationship to make the sale.

Many salespeople fall into the rut of attempting assumptive closes with their repeat customers. There certainly is some level of ease, and the sales process will be somewhat expedited, but you still need to uncover the customer's needs and provide solutions.

Use your comfort levels for ease in communication. Beyond that, you must make sure that this new sale with your old client will fill one of his needs.

# Becoming an Expert

As you move along in your sales career, there are several ways to establish yourself in your community as an expert on your industry. This is a great way to give you instant credibility as a salesperson while also reaching out to more new clients.

## Teach Classes and Seminars

Offering classes on your product, service, or industry is a great way to get your name out in the community.

Contact your local Chamber of Commerce, schools, colleges, business groups, banks, community centers, and so on and offer to give no-credit classes or seminars. The content could be based specifically on your industry, or it might be wider-reaching.

### Example 1

Bill the builder offers some do-it-yourself home-improvement classes at the local community center. Bill has the opportunity to teach people how to do certain types of home improvements on their own, solidifying him as a reputable homebuilder. Although it would be unethical for him to solicit the people in his class, they will always know they have someone to call on for larger projects. More importantly, Bill can talk about this class in his marketing materials or when he goes on sales calls to visit with homeowners.

### Example 2

Darlene works in sales as a travel agent. She offers to give a seminar on safe traveling at the local colleges and senior centers. She talks to the college students about safe spring break and summer trips and begins to solidify herself as an expert in her own industry. At the senior centers, she talks about the safety of group tours and how to watch out for thieves or other people who prey on the elderly in vacation destinations. Again, she's showing the community her expertise while also giving back.

### Example 3

David works for an Internet marketing firm. Once a month, he teaches local business owners at the Chamber of Commerce how to create simple websites. Slowly but surely, he will build the business community's confidence in his knowledge of website design and, more importantly, Internet marketing.

## Editorials

*Be local media's go-to expert in your field.*

Sales professionals of all kinds can offer up their services to the local news as a go-to expert on their industry. This could be in the form of a regular news column, on-air contributions for television or radio, or even an article in a local magazine. By being the media's go-to expert on their industry, they will in turn gain the community's trust in their expertise.

## Example 1

Sandra is a real estate agent. Every Tuesday night, one of the local television stations lets her talk about real estate on the national or local level. She talks about a hot real estate topic and gives her expert opinion. This is a win-win situation for everyone. Sandra gets a free indirect form of advertising, the station gets free content, and the public gets news or expert advice on real estate.

## Example 2

Dan is a salesman at a local electronics store. Each week, he writes an "Ask the Expert" column for the local newspaper. People write in to ask consumer technology questions, and he gives them his advice. The article always closes with, "Feel free to write to us with your questions or come visit Dan at A+ Electronics."

## Example 3

Irene sells commercial and industrial flooring for a local distributor. Due to some changes in the OSHA requirements for flooring, she offers to write an article for a local business magazine to help set the record straight. This free service will certainly help businesses make sure they are up to code, while also establishing Irene as the local go-to expert.

Continual prospecting techniques are exactly that—continual. To have success in sales, you must continue prospecting in as many ways as possible. When business is good, keep it that way by bringing in more clients using these strategies.

# Action Plan

✓ Determine how you are most comfortable asking for referrals.

✓ Decide what changes you can make to your referral script to help your clients target referrals to give you.

✓ Continually scour your database for referrals.

✓ Continually scour your database for sales with your existing clients.

✓ Lend your expertise to the community.

✓ Be sure to make prospecting a primary part of your day throughout your entire sales career.

# Chapter 9

# Industry Specifics

- Advertising
- Real Estate
- Medical
- Home Improvement and Services
- Insurance and Financial Services
- Boats, Autos, and Machinery
- Business Services and Supply
- Small-Business Owners
- Action Plan

Through this entire book, I've been speaking generally in an attempt to include most or all forms of sales positions in the conversation. This chapter is an opportunity to explore specific and popular sales industries. Many of these industries warrant an entire book on their own, but here you will find some targeted information and theories. Even if you don't work in the specific industry being discussed, you'll still get some benefit from reading each section. Some of this information can cross over into related industries, and you never know when you might want to make a change.

# Advertising

*Advertising sales offers all kinds of opportunity.*

Let's start off with my favorite of all sales industries—advertising. Full disclosure: I spent a large portion of my sales career working in advertising sales. It's a wide-ranging industry with all kinds of opportunity. Generally, in an entry-level position, anyone can get into the business, and many have fulfilling careers. You can find these positions working for radio stations, newspapers, television stations, cable companies, yellow pages, websites, search engines, magazines, direct-mail outfits, and more.

## Pros

Advertising is a great place where you can start a sales career or even complete an entire career. This is one of the few industries where you are selling your clients something that can make them quite a bit of money if done right. There's nothing more rewarding than putting together an effective marketing program and then learning that your client's phone is ringing off the hook.

Many of these positions come with a large amount of freedom. Management wants you out of the office and in front of business owners. Also, advertising sales has very straightforward goal systems. You can hit your numbers and then coast, or you can keep running and make quite a bit of money.

Some people who are uncomfortable with sales and prefer a more creative career may prefer this industry. There is some selling going on, but most sales reps play a large role in the conceptual design of the implemented marketing strategy.

## Cons

Business owners are your only clientele. Although there are some advantages to this, there is massive competition, and some business owners treat advertising expenses as if they aren't a need. If you work in radio, other radio-station sales reps will be calling on your client, as well as magazine, television, and Internet reps, and so on.

There is a very high level of turnover in advertising sales. This has a lot to do with the position generally being treated as entry level. When anyone and everyone gets a shot at business-to-business sales, there is bound to be a good bit of turnover.

Compensation is good, but it varies and fluctuates frequently based on product, customer type, and even time of year.

## What Works

If you choose a career in advertising sales, it's important that you work for a company with a product you truly believe in. It's going to be your goal to convince business owners that you can make them money with your advertising medium.

What you present to your client will be highly customizable. It's not a simple yes or no decision for your client to make. Management will frequently suggest that you come in making multiple—usually three—offers. There will be a medium plan that's right around where you think the client should be. You'll also have an over-the-top plan to make sure you leave no money on the table and then a smaller one just to make sure you get some level of business.

This tactic can work, especially for someone new to the business and sales overall. However, if you make this into a needs-based purchase, you should be able to accurately come in with one proposed marketing plan. Trying to get more money on a whim and having a parachute plan shows a lack of confidence in what you've proposed. It's very easy to make changes if a disagreement arises, so going in with a well-targeted plan is best if you have the ability.

Just as with any other business-to-business sales position, make sure you remain at the front of your customers' minds. This doesn't mean you should bog them down with phone calls all the time; just make sure they know you're out there working for them. If you fall off the radar and someone comes in with a similar or better plan, you might have to kiss your renewals goodbye.

# Real Estate

In real estate, you're selling yourself more than a product, since the property is not technically yours to sell.

Real estate is one of the true paradoxes in the world of sales. You're selling a product that isn't really yours to sell. You are brought on by homeowners as an expert to help them sell or find a home. You wear many hats as an entrepreneur, a marketing expert, a self-promoter, a market analyst—and sometimes a psychologist, depending on who you ask.

## Pros

Because it is a very entrepreneurial position, real estate sales professionals have a virtually unlimited ceiling for earnings. Like a small business, you can grow your real estate practice to whatever you choose to handle. You have all of the freedoms of other outside sales positions, and you get to work with people during a very important stage in their life. You can grow this position to any level you choose. It can be a part-time opportunity if you so choose, or you can amass a huge database of clients and bring on other agents to work below you.

## Cons

Not all real estate sales involve a happy, expectant couple approved for half a million dollars looking for a beautiful new home with a white picket fence. Many sales involve divorces, deaths, short sales and foreclosures, and so on. This can be a rough position for a highly emotional or weak-willed person.

Real estate involves many fees to the state, your broker, and different real estate boards, not to mention all of the costs associated with running a version of your own small business. Not only does this prove to be an expensive industry to get into, it's also a place where anyone can play if they pay (and pass a test).

## What Works

It's important to realize that as a real estate agent, the only selling you do is of yourself, when you signs up buyers and sellers. You are selling your ability to sell their home or to show them new homes and negotiate on their behalf. No matter what you do, you cannot really "sell" a person into a home. Price and quality dictate whether a home is a viable purchase. You are the great facilitator. Once you understand that your job is selling yourself to people looking to get into the market, you will be on track to great success.

More than in any other sales position, prospecting is your number-one concern in real estate. Many agents get bogged down or even burnt out by spending all of their time selling people into homes. Your goal is to obtain as many clients as possible. The rest isn't easy, but it will certainly fall into place if you make the right efforts. Because this position is a very entrepreneurial one, you will have the opportunity to hire people to handle other parts of the real estate process. Some of the top agents I know have agents to help their buyers, assistants, people who handle closings, other agents for open houses, and so on. The one certainty that always remains in place is that the lead agent always does the prospecting and the initial listing appointment. They are the ones selling their services to the homeowner or buyer.

When you've secured a house to sell, one of the few tangibles you can help control is the sale price. Although it's ultimately up to the homeowners, you are the expert they have brought in to help sell their home. There are two schools of thought with regard to pricing in the real estate agent's world. First, you can price the home aggressively so that it sells as quickly as possible. Second, you can price the home as high as the homeowner wants and sit back and collect buyers who call in from the sign. If you are at a comfortable place in your real estate career, a hybrid of both usually works best. Allow your client to take a shot with the price of their choice and then, after a well-defined short amount of time, trim the pricing to something aggressive enough to sell based on the current market conditions.

# Medical

Medical sales are generally pharmaceutical or medical device sales. You might be calling on private-practice doctors or servicing entire hospitals. This can be one of the most difficult industries to break into, but it's also one of the most rewarding.

The medical sales field is difficult to break into, but also very rewarding.

## Pros

Medical salespeople make, on average, more than reps in any other mainstream type of sales. This is why it is frequently a highly sought-after position. These salespeople also have an opportunity to work in a very exciting industry that most people respect and can relate to. Your customer base is well defined, so prospecting is not as crucial as it is in other sales industries. Most of what a medical sales rep does involves rapport building and education.

Most sales companies in the medical world give incentive-based pay to their salespeople and all the way up through management. Unlike other sales positions, upward movement can also result in higher earnings.

## Cons

Even though it is a difficult industry to break into, there is very little stability once you are aboard. You may earn quite a bit of money for some time, but a dry spell can quickly result in termination.

Although this position is often highly regarded as professional, some pharmaceutical companies have taken a bad rap as of late with the tumultuous world of healthcare.

Some may not see this as a con, but it serves as a warning to those who would: This position requires a lot of education once aboard. You must have clinical-level knowledge of your products because you will be educating much of your clientele. Balancing this high-level of study and knowledge with high-pressure sales can be difficult for some.

## What Works

Know your product inside and out. There is a lot of rapport building, and you have to make all kinds of sales calls, but this will all be for nothing if you don't know your product. Doctors are highly educated individuals, and they work best with those who have at least done the same with regard to the product they are selling. As much as management may push perks and poppers with your client base, you will earn the most business and respect by becoming an expert on what you are selling.

Focus on consistent business. You will make more with the bigger sales, as in any industry, but you also must maintain your base goals to keep your job security.

# Home Improvement and Services

Home improvement sales positions require a strong knowledge of the industry.

Estimators, contractors, foreman, salespeople—whatever you call them, the people showing up on homeowners' door steps to deliver proposals are working in sales. Most of these positions require a working knowledge of the specific industry. Sometimes, these salespeople are even involved in banging nails from time to time, depending on the size of the company.

## Pros

This is a great hybrid blue-collar position. You get to be in the world of home improvement and services while also earning money on an incentive-based level. You'll spend your time on the road and on a ladder, which—I'll be sexist and admit—most men enjoy.

Although incentive based, most of these positions have a substantial base salary and a car or car allowance, because much of what you are doing is related to building proposals for work.

## Cons

Unless you are the contractor, the incentive-based payments pale in comparison to those in most other sales positions. Even with the stability of a base salary, there is a bit of stability lacking in most of these positions. Also, home-improvement work can be seasonal and can be greatly affected by the economy. And, to deal with homeowners' schedules, you might be required to work evenings and weekends, unless you are with a business-to-business contractor.

## What Works

More than just getting a good price, homeowners want to do business with someone they can trust. Although price will play a role, it's important to get more caught up in the quality and/or efficiency of your company's services. Even people going with a lower price and quality will still want to at least be sure your company is going to deliver. The home-improvement world is littered with fly-by-night companies, and most people have been burned by one—or they know someone else who has.

Make sure you respond to calls and inquiries as soon as possible if this is an aspect of the business over which you have control. Even more than most other types of clients, homeowners seek out instant gratification due to their limited time in dealing with these matters.

# Insurance and Financial Services

Insurance and financial-service sales positions require licenses earned through state testing.

Again with full disclosure: This is an industry in which I did not have a great deal of success. I am professional enough to not sound jaded, and I know many people who have had great success in this field. These salespeople offer financial services to businesses and consumers, ranging from life insurance, to annuities, investments, disability, health insurance, and other benefits. These positions require different types of licenses attained through state testing.

## Pros

This position is generally a commission-only career, save for training pay or stipends. Although this may be a concern for some, it's also a sign of virtually limitless earnings. Once you have the required licenses, you can sell people and businesses almost any financial product they may need, making you a one-stop shop for your client base. This creates loyal customers and allows for multiple sales with repeat customers.

These positions usually have very low goal standards that are well defined in order for you to keep your job. This position is what you make of it, and only gross negligence or absenteeism would cause you to be fired. With the limitless earnings, people quickly either fizzle out or go on to make a substantial income.

## Cons

This is a highly regulated industry. All correspondence must be approved by a compliance officer; otherwise, you and your company can risk being fined by the SEC.

This is a very flooded industry. The promises of high earnings get many people to take a shot. Because there is little risk to the companies, they will hire as many people as possible and see who sticks. One of the qualifying factors of this position is based on how many people you know. Because advertising is highly restricted, they count on their sales force soliciting their own circle of influence.

## What Works

If you're comfortable soliciting your friends and family for business, this is an excellent position. If you're not comfortable doing so, it's important that you build a referral base out of your circle of influence. You may not want to sell an annuity to your parents, but it might be easier to ask them for a few referrals or people you can call on. As your referral base builds, you will no longer have to work within your own circle of influence. Similar to real estate, the primary concern of this position is prospecting. Once you uncover needs, the products will sell themselves.

# Boats, Autos, and Machinery

These high-end retail positions are some of the most common in the sales world. This is a very competitive market, but it can also be very lucrative.

High-end retail sales can be very lucrative, but also highly competitive.

## Pros

Boat, auto, and machinery salespeople are some of the few retail salespeople who can have a full-blown career within the industry. Mobility is high in this position, as successful salespeople can relocate or even make changes locally with ease. It's an easier industry to get into, and it's an easy one to fizzle out of, but the ones who make it are treated very well by their employers.

The pay can be good, but employers offer all kinds of incentives, bonuses, and poppers to keep the top performers happy. Because of the car-salesman stigma, referrals can go a long way. If you can sell people cars and they have a comfortable experience, they are some of the easiest people to get referrals from.

## Cons

Although all sales positions come with a stigma, none carry a tougher burden than people in the world of automobile sales. This can make it difficult to build trust or rapport with incoming clients. To top it off, these salespeople have a very short sales process considering the size of the ticket being purchased. This shortened sales process is likely what has bred the pushiness associated with some of these salespeople.

### What Works

Look past the stigma. You're helping people find the right car for the right price.

Know your product inside out and become more of a facilitator than a salesperson. Take good notes and be sure to follow up with clients who have not made buying decisions. If you treat your clients right, be sure to ask them for referrals. Also, work with your company to be sure you have the budget and ability to solicit your existing customer base. Once you've made several sales, sending customers things in the mail announcing sales or other events with your dealership will get them thinking about other people in their life looking for a car, boat, or other type of machinery.

## Business Services and Supply

Business-to-business sales can range from payroll services to supply-chain needs for manufacturing. Although the products and services range widely, they all have a similar feel in that they are business-to-business sales.

### Pros

Unlike the difficulty with advertising sales, most businesses view your products as needs. They know they need materials for production, uniforms, payroll, cleaning, employment help, and so on to keep their business running smoothly.

Business-to-business salespeople enjoy a more typical work schedule than those working with consumers or residential clients. Income can be good, and it can also be relatively steady for a sales position. Most business services operate on a continual basis, which allows the salesperson to build his own bottom line.

### Cons

Any business-to-business industry can be extremely competitive. Because four other people are trying to sell a similar product, your time and access may be limited initially during the prospecting phase. Although there is potential for very competitive earnings, there is somewhat of a cap on earnings based on the amount of service required to keep business relationships working.

## What Works

Prospecting will get you started early in your business-to-business sales career, but that will shift over to service depending on how quickly you get to your personal capacity.

Focus your initial prospecting on businesses with obvious and defined needs. They may be the most over-solicited, but they are for a reason. Focus on some of the fringe businesses that may not have been contacted once you're up and running. When you're close to capacity, it is easy to rely on referrals for any further new business you may seek out.

# Small-Business Owners

If you own a small business, you are a salesperson on some level. You may have become an accountant because you love math, but you're going to have to do a bit of selling if you want to go out on your own. In the business world, selling is better known as marketing and advertising.

## Pros

More so than any other position we've talked about, your earnings are limitless and your freedom is ultimate, as you answer only to yourself. (I can see all you husbands and wives out there shaking your heads....)

In other sales positions, you are somewhat restricted to working in unison with your company's overall strategy. As a business owner, you dictate your own strategy. You can implement marketing plans and seek out new business in a variety of ways. You can grow your company as large as your customer base will qualify.

## Cons

In no other sales position do you risk more. Business owners are fully responsible for funding themselves, and failure can result in massive debts, not a simple firing. Although it's not quite as competitive as some sales positions, depending on what industry you get into, the business world is known for its competitiveness.

There is no guarantee, base salary, or goals set forth by anyone else. There is no formula provided to you that can guarantee success. There is not even a general plan of action available to you, as opposed to a traditional sales position, with well-defined goals and earnings.

## What Works

First and foremost, pick up a copy of my other book, *90 Days to Success Marketing and Advertising Your Small Business* (Course Technology PTR, 2010).

In all seriousness, marketing is truly the key to a successful business. Marketing is the business owner's version of sales. Marketing helps with the prospecting, as it brings people to you—then it becomes your job to convert them into clients.

Make sure you're starting your business well funded and that you include money for advertising. Treat your new business position as a sales position. Uncover people's needs and meet them with your services. Ask for referrals. Grow to the capacity your business is capable of handling.

# Action Plan

✓ Determine how your sales position differs from those found in other industries.

✓ Determine how it is similar to those in other industries.

✓ Work to become more educated about your industry and your competition.

✓ Determine the pros and cons of your current position.

✓ Focus on the pros and deal with the cons.

# Chapter 10

# The Life of a Salesperson

- Personal Finance
- Mental and Physical Health
- Automobiles
- Appearance
- Vacations
- Mixing Business and Pleasure
- Hobbies
- Community Involvement
- Employment Opportunities
- Action Plan

The way you live your personal life plays a major role in your success in sales. I believe this to be one of the most overlooked topics by sales management, sales trainers, and other authors writing about sales. Having worked in sales, with plenty of highs and lows both personally and professionally, I can tell you it has every bit to do with your successes. Your personal finances must be under control to handle the ebb and flow of sales income, especially in the earliest phases. Even your mental and physical health play a role in building a successful sales career.

## Personal Finance

*Aside from your professional life, personal finance plays the most important role in your sales success.*

Personal finance plays the most important part of your success in sales, outside of your professional life. It's important for you to get your finances under control, not just to survive the uncertainty of pay, but also to keep your emotions in check through the entire sales process.

A lack of personal funds can affect your sales ability in some obvious ways. Financial desperation is hard to hide during the sales process. Being desperate for the sale makes you less likely to fill your clients' needs and more likely to go for the easiest and fastest road to a sale. In addition to you delivering a rushed and ill-informed sales process, some clients will even be able to pick up on your unusual demeanor.

Part of working in a sales position involves operating like a small business. If you don't have room in your budget for the basics, you're going to sell yourself short on time and effort. Salespeople need money for travel, coffee or other entertainment with clients, events, cell phones, and other supplies not provided by their employer. Even if you manage to just barely squeak by in your personal life, cutting corners will show in your professional life.

On a darker note, some may even be lured into forms of sales fraud due to desperation. Not only will actions like that cost you your job, they can lead to civil or criminal prosecution.

Believe it or not, a wealth of funds can also have a negative effect on your sales ability. I'm not telling you to turn down money or that financial success is a burden, but it *can* create a sense of complacency with your sales process. This can be especially true for people newer to the world of sales. For many people, sales success might be one of their first experiences with having a large amount of money in the bank. Someone going from paycheck to paycheck for most of his professional career to a sales position that leaves him with thousands of dollars in the bank might find himself feeling a little too comfortable with a little less effort.

*Too much money can affect your sales ability negatively, just as too little money can.*

The newfound wealth might tempt some to splurge and spend like they never have in the past. How many times have you heard about a professional athlete making millions of dollars, only to go bankrupt just a short time out of a league? The same thing can happen in any other career in which people are met with a surge of money they're not used to dealing with. Sales can provide a better life for some, as long as your finances are well managed.

## Income Management

There are many ways in which a well-disciplined salesperson can learn to live within her means. This doesn't require a whole lot of sacrifice, nor does it mean you have to keep your hands off your hard-earned money. This section provides some ideas for managing a sales income.

*If you're disciplined, you can learn to live within your means on a sales income.*

People working on straight commission are generally considered 1099 contracted employees. You are responsible for your own taxes and are treated much like a subcontractor. You can write off quite a bit more than other salespeople, but you do carry the burden of far more personal responsibility.

One of the best ways to handle the ups and downs of a straight-commission position is by paying yourself a salary.

As a new salesperson or a seasoned veteran, you should have a realistic idea of what you expect to earn for the year. Remember, this is a *realistic*, low-ball number, not the loftiest of your personal goals. When you have this number established, set up a separate bank account to handle your business income and expenses.

Every week, pay yourself half of your average weekly income, based on what you earn in a year. This money is for your personal expenses. The other half remains for your business expenses.

Take whatever your expected income is for the year and pay yourself half of what that works out to on a weekly or biweekly basis. If you're going to make a minimum of $52,000 for the year, you should take a salary of $500 per week (half of $52,000 divided by 52 weeks). No matter how things are going, take that $500 and put it into your personal finances. When you've had a dry spell, take the income. When you've gotten way ahead, take the same income.

Charge any business expense you have to your business account, above and beyond your $500 paycheck. If you have a client meal that will be written off, use the account. If you have a class or a licensing fee that needs to be paid for, use the account. The $500 paycheck is for your personal life. This is for groceries, entertainment, clothes—anything not related to your business life.

This will help you maintain stability in several ways. First, you will have kept enough money aside for taxes at the end of the year. You'll also have your business expenses closely tracked by using the account, so putting together your write-offs will be easy at the end of the year. You can pay yourself any leftover money as a "bonus" at the end of the year. These (hopefully) large sums can go toward down payments on a house or car, retirement, or anything you see fit—it's your money! Just be sure to leave enough of a cushion in the account to deal with any downs you might start the year with.

As you move forward in your sales career, feel free to revisit these numbers. You may end up targeting a much higher income. Other years, it may go down.

If you need access to the bonus money any sooner, consider evaluating your account quarterly or every month and giving yourself bonuses then. Just be sure to consult with an accountant or a tax professional to be sure you're on track for your quarterly estimated taxes.

For those of you paid as an employee with any level of a base salary, you can adhere to a similar plan. Depending on how large your base salary is, you can plan to "pay" yourself that salary along with a fixed amount of income from your anticipated commissions each pay period. Remember, you will not have to save as much, because your employer will be taking out taxes all year long. That being said, the more you can save, the better.

The simplest way to manage your finances is to treat a sales process the way some people treat the potential for unemployment. You might be a good salesperson and make a good amount of income each year, but in some sales careers, a month or more without pay isn't unheard of.

A simple safety net of three, six, or nine months of salary should give you a nice cushion in the event of a sales drought or, worse yet, being fired. These may sound like large numbers, but trust me, money goes quickly when you don't have any coming in to replace it.

> Have a safety net of three, six, or nine months of salary in savings, in case of a sales drought or layoff.

Do your best to keep your hands off these emergency funds so that they'll be available if or when you need them.

## Savings and Retirement

As with most other careers, some sales positions offer assistance with retirement, and others do not. When you are a straight commissioned salesperson with no investment options with your employer, it is of crucial importance that you come up with a plan for retirement. With no easy investments or pensions, your cash saved is the only thing you're left with when you retire. Investing ensures that your cash will grow while it's waiting for you.

> Be sure to establish a retirement plan if you're a salesperson on straight commission.

Contract-type employees often overlook the fact that they have many aggressive and tax-friendly options for investments that are identical to those offered to small-business owners. Ask your accountant or a financial professional about the benefits of a SEP retirement account and other retirement options usually set aside for the self-employed.

You can enjoy the freedom you have grown to love in your sales position during retirement—and at a much sooner pace than most if you plan accordingly.

## Startup Money

At the beginning of any sales career, it can take considerable time to get clients into the pipeline, turn them into sales, and get paid. Without a base salary, some positions may take a month or more to yield even the slightest results.

> Some sales positions take a month or more to yield financial results.

When I started my first sales job, I didn't have any concept of how long it would take to be paid for sales I had turned in. In my first two weeks, I had thousands of dollars in commissioned sales. I was living up to the edge of my budget when I opened my first check, which included only my base pay for two weeks—just a shade over $600.

It is not a good idea to take on a sales position without having a comfortable cushion of money to live on until your commissions start paying off. However, I understand that this is real life, and you're not always able to have these perfect circumstances.

Although it might detract from your initial sales efforts, it may be fiscally responsible for you to take on some additional part-time work. It might be a lot of hours at first, but once you're up and running, you can let go of the additional work if you see fit.

## Mental and Physical Health

Most sales positions require a fair amount of mental and even physical stamina. The stresses of fluctuating income, high-pressure sales situations, frequent travel, and obscene multitasking requirements can take their toll.

*To avoid burnout, you must work smart and incorporate personal time into your schedule.*

Mental health in a sales position is all about balance. You are working in sales to facilitate your personal life. Your earnings go toward improving your overall life experience while providing for your family. This is all in vain if you don't take the time to enjoy the things you are working so hard for. Also, spending countless hours in the office or in front of clients will cause you to burn out. Some burn out more quickly than others, but it *will* happen. Hard work is great, but you must also learn to work smart and incorporate personal time into your schedule.

Salespeople face rejection on a day-to-day basis. It might be easy to take it for a while, but it's important to make sure you don't let your failures and rejections get you down. This downward spiral can have an effect on the rest of your otherwise positive sales experiences if you don't keep it in check. Learn to get your mind off work each night so that you can recharge and get over the day's failures.

Mounting pressure can also have an adverse effect on your mental health: pressure to perform, pressure to provide, and pressure from your clients. Learn how to deal with these pressures and how to release yourself from them at the day's end.

These mental burdens are a very serious matter. If you feel as if things are getting out of control, talk to someone you work with. If it's moved beyond that and has infected your personal life, seek professional help. Salespeople have one of the highest suicide rates of any type of professionals in the United States.

Staying in good physical health will translate into better efficiency in the workplace. Eating well and making time for physical activity will help you have the energy it takes to get through a strenuous sales day without crashing by the time you get home.

Everyone knows the benefits of good physical health, and most people can understand how this would affect workplace efficiency. The difference between workplace efficiency in a typical job versus in a sales position is money in your pocket. When you have the ability to control your income, you want to do everything you can to maximize your efficiency.

Given the level of freedom that most salespeople have, joining a gym is a great idea. You can work out at typical times before or after work, but many salespeople choose to get in a workout midday because of a lull in their schedule. Also, gyms are a great place to find new potential leads to conduct business with!

# Automobiles

If you work in outside sales, you'll need reliable transportation. One of the biggest shocks to new salespeople is how many miles you can end up putting on your car. Gas mileage is important to most people, but it will play an even more important role in your personal finances if you are filling up every other day.

New salespeople are often surprised at the number of miles they put on their car each month.

Most leases allow for what amounts to about 1,000 miles per month. Even in some localized sales positions, you can easily triple that number. Be sure to recognize the number of miles you will be putting on your car before you sign a lease or buy a brand-new car. Durability, gas mileage, and any amount of sustained value in a car are the top things to consider when you are purchasing a car to be used for outside sales.

Many sales positions require you to transport marketing materials, literature, samples, leave-behinds, and so on, so be sure to consider this before opting for a subcompact car that's good on gas.

# Appearance

You're not supposed to judge a book by its cover, but the cover is what gets you to pick it up in the first place, right?

You don't need to be a supermodel to have success in sales. You don't need a $3,000 suit, either. That being said, what you show on the outside can be somewhat of a reflection of what's going on inside. You'd think much of this would go without saying, but I've seen many salespeople work in wrinkled shirts, with unkempt hair, and a couple even in pajamas. Some leave you with no doubt in your mind that they haven't bathed in days. A more politically correct person might tell you that these things don't matter, but the truth is, for better or worse, they do.

*Dress professionally but not ostentatiously, and always be well groomed.*

The opposite can sometimes be true, too. Focusing on your appearance too much and living up to the flashy salesperson stigma will leave people judging you, just as they judge those on the other end of the spectrum. Be professional and take pride in your appearance.

# Vacations

In most sales positions, there is no such thing as a true vacation. You simply cannot manage a book of business while being totally cut off from the world for more than a few days.

*It's nearly impossible to take a true vacation of more than a couple of days when you have a sales position. Resign yourself to doing a bit of work even while on vacation.*

Vacations are a very important part of many people's lives. It can be enriching for your family and the perfect escape for you and your loved ones. The best way to take extended vacations from work is by accepting that you will have to do some minimal level of calling and emailing while you're away. If you share this with your family in advance, it will help everyone to accept it.

Plan your vacations well in advance and be sure to take care of as many of your duties as possible before you leave. If you have access to a company assistant or you have a friend who can cover a few things for you, it's fine to leave things to people you are comfortable with.

Although there is no way to know what may come up in your absence, plan on spending an hour or less per day dealing with work-related issues. This hour can be tucked away into any lull you may have during the day.

This window can even be a specific hour where you are semi-working. With today's technology, it's easy to take calls and check email while you are on the go, enjoying your vacation. Tell your co-workers and active clients that the only time to reach you on vacation will be from, say, 2 to 3 p.m. Take your calls and emails then if they come in, but be sure to shut off your phone outside that timeframe!

*While on vacation, shut off your phone except during designated hours when you are available to take business calls.*

It might sound like a drag to accept some level of work responsibility when on vacation, but if you own up to it and realize that it will be profitable in the long run, a small amount of time each day will not prevent you from recharging while on vacation.

## Mixing Business and Pleasure

I'll keep this section rated PG, but this is a topic worth delving into. While most people have a level of social interaction with their co-workers, people in the sales world have a turbo-charged version of what the rest of the world's workforce experiences.

Salespeople spend a large amount of time in mixed social settings with their co-workers and clients. These situations can include luncheons, dinners, parties, drinks, social events, and even trips. Experiences like these build team camaraderie as well as rapport with your company's clientele.

It's important to let your hair down and let people see a bit of the "real" you. At the same time, you must also remember that these people are your co-workers and clients. Whether you choose to be a casual drinker or not is up to your discretion, but be sure you know your limits. Besides the obvious safety issues, you also have to deal with the repercussions of alcohol-fueled mistakes.

*If you choose to drink at social events related to your sales career, know your limits. Getting drunk in front of your co-workers or clients won't do you any favors.*

Interoffice relationships can also make sense, considering the amount of time salespeople spend together personally and professionally. Just keep in mind that if a relationship doesn't work out, you still have to work together in a professional work environment.

Remember that rumors spread quickly in any office environment, and the last thing you want to do is make a mistake that will cause you or someone else continual discomfort in the workplace.

# Hobbies

A successful sales career can reward you with a life of financial wealth and freedom. However, although you may have a legitimate interest in your particular industry, sales jobs often lack the same sense of reward that goes along with other professional careers. With careers in medicine, education, the arts, and even construction or legal services, people tend to have a higher sense of accomplishment. They're helping people directly, and the fruits of their efforts can be seen in a much more immediate, day-to-day way.

With a sales career, it can be easy to burn out if you have no way to fill this void. I have seen a fair number of highly successful salespeople step away from their career simply because they did not feel as if they were making a difference. You can certainly spend time reaffirming the importance of your sale, but a great way to add completeness to your life is by picking up a hobby or pursuing your other life interests.

Because of the freedom and higher income that comes along with a sales role, these positions are great for people whose true passions lie outside of a traditional career path. Your income can help you sustain interests and hobbies of all kinds, and the typical flexibility of a sales schedule can help you pursue them.

When I worked as an advertising sales executive in Los Angeles, I did get some personal satisfaction from the successes I helped business owners find through advertising. However, I became an avid mountain climber to add to my overall quality of life. After a rough week of work, I might spend a Friday afternoon hiking in the nearby Angeles National Forest. With my extra income from a particularly large commission check, I might plan a trip with friends for a climb in Northern California or somewhere to the south, in Mexico.

These extracurricular passions help promote balance in your life and keep you from burning out in a fast-paced and sometimes less personally rewarding environment.

Personal goals within your hobby or outside interests can help drive your success in sales as well. We're all motivated by the savings and security a nice commission check can provide, but there's nothing wrong with an avid sailor being motivated by the need for a new sail or an amateur botanist wanting to travel to a lush rainforest!

## Community Involvement

Getting involved in the community is a great way to get your name out in the public while also doing something rewarding. Joining a committee or being on a board of directors will give you an extra sense of accomplishment while bolstering your sales career.

Getting involved in the community can be personally and professionally rewarding.

People want to do business with people they already associate with on another level. Giving back to the community will give you a chance to refocus and recharge while creating a little extra presence to help you along in your sales career. Remember, most salespeople do what they do for the freedom and financial reward. This can allow you to focus on other things you're passionate about. These extracurricular activities may be some of the things you've sought all along.

## Employment Opportunities

Depending on what stage of your career you find yourself in, it's important to keep an eye open to improving your career with a change in employment.

I'm not telling you to give up all loyalty to your current position; just be open-minded that it might lead to new opportunities and challenges. You may impress some of your clients so much that they want to consider you for employment with their company or suggest that you interview where they work.

Nothing can kill a resume more than a bunch of short-term jumping around, but it's understood that people need to look elsewhere for growth from time to time. If you can handle several years with any given position, you'll be in better shape than someone who has to count the number of months they've worked in most positions.

Although this might seem hard to grasp if you're early in your career, understand that you may spend the rest of your working life with your current company. Look around you. If there are successful people there with decades of experience with the same company and suitable earnings to qualify their decision, why not consider it for yourself?

# Action Plan

✓ Make sure your finances are intact and will support the beginning of your sales career.

✓ Don't let your personal finances affect your sales process.

✓ Decide what ways you can steady your income to create more balance in your personal finances.

✓ Make a plan to save for retirement.

✓ Make sure your mental and physical health are in check.

✓ Make sure your car is appropriate for your specific sales position.

✓ Take pride in the way you look every day.

✓ Plan a vacation!

✓ Decide how you can balance your vacation time with a minimal amount of work interruption.

✓ Make sure you are well received at your company's social events.

✓ Get involved in your community.

✓ Think about your long-term career goals.

# Chapter 11

# Sales Management

- Management
- Making the Move to Management
- Laying the Groundwork
- Interviewing for a Management Position
- Other Internal Moves
- Sales Management 101
- Action Plan

This chapter is divided into three sections. First, we'll get a bird's-eye view of management's function in the sales process. Second, we'll look into what it takes to make the move from sales to management. Finally, we'll discuss some basic management strategy.

All three of these sections are important, regardless of whether you're considering management. They will all help improve your relationship with your management, and they will also leave you with a better understanding of their methods and intentions. Although you might not be looking into management, management skills can help anytime you're in a team setting.

# Management

Most salespeople deal with some level of management. Although your relationship with your manager can be strained based on performance, it's important to remember that you're both on the same team. Having a better idea of what managers do will help you to develop a better idea of their roles and responsibilities.

## Management Roles

A manager's number-one goal is always to get his salespeople to perform well.

The number-one goal for managers in every industry is to get their salespeople to perform to the best of their abilities. Some take different paths to this goal, but they're all after the same thing.

Part of your manager's job involves facilitation. She wants to provide you with the tools and training so you'll know your product inside out and sell it with efficiency. Take full advantage of her role as your support person, and you will have the tools you need to sell your product or service. In this sense, managers can help you compile marketing information and also give you assistance in building a proposal.

Managers usually like to help you personally with the sales process. This can be especially helpful to new salespeople or those new to the industry. It might feel as if you're teaming up on your clients, but your manager's experience can pay off in sales as well as in educational experiences. Even the most experienced salesperson might bring a manager along on a difficult or an important sales call.

Motivation toward reaching goals is one of a sales manager's main functions. Depending on your manager's style this can come across through anything from encouragement to downright fear. Motivation can sometimes border on micromanaging. When it feels as if a manager is getting too involved in your business, it may be her version of pushing you toward your goals.

No matter what role your manager is playing at the time, it's important to have an open line of communication. The facilitator might be great, but maybe you're getting bogged down with a little too much information. Other times, a simple request for more support is all it takes for a manager to step up in her role as facilitator. When your manager wants to help on a sales call, it may or may not be the best fit, based on what you know about your client. There may also be times when you have to reach out for that ride-along help. The motivational portion of management's duties may be more difficult to control, even through effective communication. Rest assured, if your numbers are where they should be, most managers will respond when you ask for a bit of breathing room. No matter what you seek from your manager, be sure to communicate your needs.

## Management Compensation

You might be surprised to learn that many managers do not make more than their top salespeople. Management is a skill almost entirely separate from sales. This is why some companies have a more secure income structure for their management team. That being said, most have some form of bonuses involved, based on their team's performance. Your motivation to sell is to make money. Your manager's motivation to get you to sell is also to make money.

Many managers make less than their top salespeople.

A good manager will be transparent about his compensation. His entire sales force can calculate to the penny what each sales rep makes, based on commission rates and public sales numbers. As much as we should look to our managers as guides, we should also look to them as colleagues who we want to watch succeed. If we know their compensation plan, we can work even harder to make sure everyone reaches his goals.

The way in which managers are compensated explains why they sometimes have a sense of frustration when people aren't hitting their numbers. Yes, the obvious fact is that your manager may not make his bonus, but the difficulty in his job is his indirect way of taking action. As a salesperson, you can go out and sell more when your numbers are waning. As a sales manager, your only option is to formulate ways to keep your salespeople marching forward. This lack of direct control certainly can be frustrating, especially when it is tied to someone's variable income.

Some sales managers are still allowed to sell to select clients based on upper management's discretion. They usually are compensated in the same way as the sales force. On the plus side, their expertise and experience can help keep key clients on board. On the other hand, a sales manager who spends a large amount of time selling may have a personal conflict of interests.

## Hiring

Hiring a stable workforce is a large part of a sales manager's job.

Hiring is the largest role a manager plays that does not directly affect her current sales force. Managers have to weed through countless resumes to fill frequently open positions that come as a result of high turnover. Some of your manager's bonuses are tied into retention rate. If she brings in a stable workforce, she is rewarded. The paradox of this demand is that a salesperson looking for work is by definition at an unstable point in his career.

This stability factor is why many sales positions advertise themselves as not requiring previous sales experience. Good managers know that the experienced journeymen salespeople are not the ones who are likeliest to stick around. They are sometimes willing to trade expertise for the potential of a longer shelf life. Weighing these options while trying to build an effective sales force can be challenging.

## Upper Management

You know that guy who's in your office once every couple of weeks? The one who has your manager scurrying around the office as if he's getting ready for the second coming? That guy belongs to upper management.

Upper management consists of regional managers, directors, and vice presidents. Your managers keep you on track, and their managers do the same for them.

Upper managers supervise your direct managers.

These high-level managers handle the macro-management of the sales force. They look at big-picture numbers and simplify sales numbers into regional and/or office-by-office figures. Your interaction may be limited to quick conversations when they visit, appearances and yearly meetings, and awards, along with the occasional mass mailing to the sales force.

This level of management is compensated somewhat differently from your own manager. Upper managers have some incentive-based bonuses on the regions or territories they oversee. Most of their earnings are based on the company's overall earnings. They may be involved in a profit-sharing program paid out in bonuses or company stock and dividends.

These upper managers might just be a blip on the radar to you and your current career. However, keep in mind that these people have done a lot to get where they have in their careers. More important, it's crucial that you are in good standing with them if you ever want to be considered for management down the road. They are the ones who will re-interview you at the time, and there's a lot they'll be looking for.

As a salesperson motivated by income, you should certainly be motivated to move into upper management if you have even the slightest bit of interest. It's fairly common for local managers to make less than some of their top salespeople. So what's their motivation to drive and inspire their sales force to greatness? Upper-management income.

Not too far removed from a pyramid scheme, levels of management share in the profitability of those working below them. Your local managers may be somewhat motivated by performance bonuses, but the people they're working for often rely solely on overall company profitability.

Regional and district managers, vice presidents—however you company labels them—generally work with a system of compensation through profit sharing. This massive income is not for naught, and sometimes there isn't even a guarantee.

These men and women must pay attention to industry trends, hire and fire managers, micromanage underperforming offices, and even answer to investors. The workload certainly qualifies the income, but it is also driven by the paths necessary to achieve upper-management status.

If you have grand desires to make it to the top, following the basic steps to a management role will set you on the right path. However, most upper-management positions require time-tested experience, big numbers, and additional education. In a later chapter, we will discuss continued education, but it's worth mentioning that an MBA provides a solid starting point for anyone looking to get into upper management.

In my own experience, I watched a gentleman make the climb into upper management. He became a local sales manager after 12 years of sales experience in the field. While he was working as my manager, he acquired his MBA. Because managers have the ability to hold more true to a 9-to-5 schedule than their sales force, he was able to accomplish this educational goal through night classes. Three years after I started working for him, he was a regional sales manager, making just slightly more than the president of the United States.

# Making the Move to Management

There comes a point in every successful salesperson's career where she is asked the famous question, "Have you ever considered getting into management?"

The ever-obliging go-getter of a salesperson is always quick with an affirmative response—and then she goes about her day wondering whether she really meant it.

A move into management is a serious one to consider. The stress of day-to-day sales morphs into the stress of keeping tabs on your sales force while promoting their success and bringing new members on board. The challenges are different, and what it takes to succeed might not always be found simply in sales numbers.

# Laying the Groundwork

Having great sales numbers is initially an important part of your consideration for a management position. You have to prove you know what it's like to be out there in the field and be successful.

Strong sales numbers are a good first step to moving into a management position.

Sales success and success in sales management is not an apples-to-apples comparison. The top salespeople don't necessarily translate into the best managers. At the same time, people with numbers at the bottom of the heap with some signs of leadership have a hard time getting considered.

Once your sales numbers are on track and you are at least hitting your goals, you can sit down for the management talk. If this is something you're interested in, know that your managers are looking at several things in your overall performance.

I've mentioned that they look at numbers, but they need to know whether you have what it takes to be a leader. Are you the kind of person who is naturally drawn to helping your peers, even if there is no financial incentive? Of course, you would have financial incentives as a manager, but it still takes some natural desire to lead.

Support your peers and share ideas for success. Lift them up when they are down and congratulate them when they are up. This may be work for some of you, but others do this naturally anyway.

Take the lead first or when no one else will. This means sharing your sales numbers first when no one wants to, stepping up to role playing during continued education, or taking on assignments that might not have any defined financial value.

To demonstrate your management potential, be supportive of your peers and take the lead when others don't want to.

Now, I don't want you to start looking like a brown-noser who's deep into all of your peers' business. Management and upper management like someone who can get along, but they've been around long enough to know when someone has ulterior motives.

Take an active role in your office's training program. Much of what managers do is prepare the newer sales force to go out into the field. If you show a natural ability to teach, this is another positive factor you have going for you when it comes to consideration for a sales management position.

# Interviewing for a Management Position

You've successfully laid the groundwork to be considered for a management position. Your bosses ask you the question again, but this time you have a much deeper conversation about your career aspirations in management.

When you've told them that you're serious about taking the leap, there are several ways the interview process will work.

First, your management likely will give you some managerial assignments to see how well you can meet them with your peers. You might be instructed to lead a very directed sales push. You will be responsible for building some short-term goals qualified through simple competitive spirit in the office, and they will see whether you can lead your team to victory.

Next, managers will have you do ride-alongs with some of the newer sales staff. They want to see how well you can help newer staff through the sales process. Obviously, your managers won't be present throughout the entire sales call, so much of your success will be based on the success of the salesperson with whom you are paired.

When you've shown you have the ability to lead and nurture, your managers might have you sit in on or even conduct some interviews with potential new hires. This likely will be well scripted, as anyone doing hiring is also responsible for enticing new hires to join the fold. Your managers will have another meeting with the potential new hire, so they will be judging you on your ability to sniff out talent and turn away the duds. Be a reasonable person, and remember that you were once on the other side of that table!

*Having a good rapport with upper management will make your interview for a management position go more smoothly.*

Finally, you will need to endure a formal interview with upper management. This is why it's important to keep yourself on their radar (for positive things!) as you build your sales career. If they already have good rapport with you, the interview will go much more smoothly.

Expect this interview to be more in depth than your initial hire. While sales forces are less stringent about whom they bring in to sales (in the hopes that *some* new hires will stick), they take management hires very seriously. They are looking for people who intend to stay with the company for a long time and who can help them grow as a whole. Remember, it's the managers who are usually considered for internal promotions to upper management.

You will be drilled on your commitment as well as challenged to sort out a variety of hypothetical scenarios. Management crises are not all tied to underperforming salespeople. They need to know how you will react to a variety of challenges before they can be certain you can handle the role of a manager.

# Other Internal Moves

Not everyone making waves as a salesperson wants to or has the ability to move into management. Look around the company, and you will see many other options if and when you decide to move on from sales. Salespeople are well suited to make the move to several other areas than management.

## Marketing Positions

As you become an expert in your company's product or service, you might be considered for a role in marketing. As a marketing specialist or manager, you will develop marketing tools to help assist in the sales force's success. You might help launch new products or educate salespeople on some of the features and benefits of what they're selling.

Marketing specialists and managers educate salespeople on the products or services they're selling and help launch new products.

Some marketing roles are directed outward to the public. Even though your company has a sales force working to push your product or service, they also spend some amount of money on marketing and advertising to their consumers.

As an expert on your company's product, you can help direct the message being sent to potential clients. You know from your experiences in the field what they're looking for and what they need to hear.

## Support Staff

Some people enjoy their company but simply want to get out of sales. They may take a step back in pay, but they still have a chance to contribute to the company's overall success. They're also able to trade in the uncertainty of a commission-based salary for something a little more stable.

Your experiences set you up as an excellent sales assistant, underwriter, receptionist, or other clerical position. It might seem like a step back for some, while others will enjoy the opportunity to stay with the company even if they had wavering numbers.

## Trainers

Most large sales forces have people employed as full-time trainers. Their duties can range from training new hires in intensive initial training to conducting in-field training sessions and providing continuing education.

Trainers have an important role in any sales company's success.

This is an excellent alternative for people considering management, who would rather give up some of the numerical stresses and focus on helping individual salespeople. Trainers play an obvious but crucial role in any sales company's success.

Taking a position as a sales trainer may require you to relocate to your company's headquarters or training facility. If you're with a national company, they tend to bring people to one central location for extended training sessions.

# Sales Management 101

This is a much larger topic that deserves more than a section of a chapter in a book, but it's important that I at least touch upon this information to give you a clearer picture of what lies ahead and how you can have some initial successes.

You never know how quickly you will be asked to move into management, so it's important to be prepared in advance. Your managers may be making moves in the near future, or perhaps company expansion is imminent.

## Developing Goals

One of your first duties as a sales manager will be to develop the goal structure for your sales force. Just as you once answered to your manager for numbers, you will now answer to a new level of management for your team's overall numbers. Upper management will help you get a grasp of what they're trying to accomplish as you meld that to your plans for your sales force. They will monitor your activity and leave the successes and failures to your individual actions with your sales force.

One of the top reasons why salespeople make good sales managers is because they've been there before. They know what goals are realistic. They know what it's like to struggle to keep up. A manager experienced in sales will be able to speak to the salesperson's concerns about goals much better than someone hired from an outside firm will.

*A salesperson's experience in the trenches is a big part of what makes him an effective sales manager.*

Keep in mind that the goals you develop for your sales staff are the same ones upper management will hold you accountable to. If you set goals too low just so that your team can hit them, your overall profitability may not be what they're looking for. If you set them too high and your team misses them, the morale of your sales force will be shredded.

Most upper management will give you a set of goals that you also need to achieve through the manipulation of your own goal system. You might find that setting goals a few points higher than where they need you to be will be your safest bet. Your sales force will have something to strive for, and even if they come up a few points short, you should reach your managerial goals.

## Hiring

You've known it all along. I've told you about it throughout this book, and you've come to realize it in your own experiences. Sales managers will hire almost anyone. Now it's your turn to do the hiring.

Upper management might give you a bit of a budget to go out and find new hires. You can place ads, attend job fairs, or even work with an employment agency. No matter the route, you're the one who will be sitting across from the fresh faces, confirming that they have a pulse.

In time, you will get it. In time, you will see that the transient sales workforce isn't filled with all the top performers you were hoping for. You'll have to take risks based on hunches to find the right people to add to your sales force. Many will come, but few will stay.

*Follow your hunches to find the right people to add to your team.*

No matter how you elect to do your hiring, keep in mind that you have to do what's best for your company. If it's getting a bunch of bodies out in the field, you're going to have to oblige. Screen people for red flags that imply they may scam or rip off clientele and make sure you're comfortable with the person sitting across the table representing your company.

## Facilitation and Training

You're an expert in your field by now, so share your knowledge with your team.

Part of your consideration for a management position was based on your product knowledge. You've become an expert in your field, and now it's time for you to share your mental wealth with other salespeople.

New hires obviously will need the most help. They've gone through some level of formal training, but you are their go-to person when they are out getting real-world experience.

Know your marketing materials so that you can help your salespeople become familiar with their products. Help them uncover their own customers' needs and then play a hand in tailoring a solution.

Some of your salespeople will want or require some help on sales calls. It's important to have a game plan in place with your salesperson before you go into the meeting. Are you going to run things, or are you going to sit there and answer some of the more difficult questions? Are you going to play the role of sales manager, or are you being brought in as a product expert?

## Motivation

One of the most difficult managerial tasks is figuring out how to rally the troops. For some reason still unknown to me, people need more than just money as an incentive to perform.

Holding sales meetings and giving recognition are common ways managers reward their employees. Cheer on the top salespeople and make their experience something that new or underperforming salespeople aspire to share.

Use sales games and contests to help motivate your sales force.

Creating sales games and contests might feel as if you're getting third-graders to complete an assignment, but most people respond well to a little light-hearted competition among their peers. Most managers have a budget set aside for such events, whether the awards are bonuses or other kinds of prizes.

Spend one-on-one time with your employees outside of your regularly scheduled meetings. A lunch to catch up as friends and talk a bit of business can lift people's spirits. Believe it or not, there's usually a budget set aside for this as well.

## Discipline

Discipline can be one of the most difficult parts of your role as a sales manager. Salespeople are going to fail you. In fact, a majority of salespeople are going to fail you. There is a high turnaround in most sales positions, so you can't take these issues to heart. Some people will just quit on you, but others will have to endure your discipline and even be fired.

Some salespeople will simply underachieve. You might try your hardest to teach and motivate them, but it just doesn't work out. At this point, you have to figure out whether they are still worth managing or if the dead weight is bringing down the rest of the sales team.

Sometimes a jarring will get them back on course:

> "Jim, your numbers have been poor for several months now, and I think we both need to make a decision about your future here. What do you want to do?"

Straightforward tactics are much better than blind-siding someone with a pink slip. It was important for you to be honest with your manager when you were a salesperson, and now it's important for you to be honest with your employees.

Some levels of discipline come up over issues of gross negligence. Some of your employees may wrong their customers for their own gain. Others will take part in unacceptable office behavior. It's important for you to set the bar as early as you can and stick to it to keep your employees away from some of the more negligent and even sometimes criminal activities.

*Salespeople will fail you, so part of your job will include discipline.*

## Compensation

As tough as these new challenges may be, companies take care of good managers. They've put in a lot of time grooming you as a salesperson and then moving you into a management position, after all.

You most likely will have a base salary tied to some incentive-based bonuses. Be sure to iron out the details before you sign on to avoid any surprises. As with a sales position, make sure you are financially sound before making the move into sales management.

I once had a sales manager who made a salary of $26,000. At the end of each year, he was bonused into the six-figure range.

## Action Plan

✓ Make sure you have a working knowledge of your manager's roles and responsibilities.

✓ Understand that your manager is goal driven as well and is human!

✓ Think about how you can help your manager reach his or her personal goals.

✓ Try to position yourself as a candidate for management.

✓ Prepare for your initial testing and interviews for a management position.

✓ Determine how your compensation would change as a manager.

✓ Get educated in the world of management if you plan to make the move!

# Chapter 12

# Retail Sales

- Retail Careers and Compensation
- Prospecting
- Rapport Building
- Needs Analysis
- Presentation and Solution
- Closing
- Retail Sales Positions
- Action Plan

A majority of this book has focused on sales with a long to medium sales process. It is far easier to break down the sales process when there is time involved. Retail sales, however, takes the entire sales process (which can last for weeks) and compresses it into something that can amount to less than half an hour.

In this chapter, we will compare and contrast the short sales process of retail sales versus the lengthier traditional sales process. Regardless of whether you work in retail, you can learn by studying the retail sales process. Many sales positions are a hybrid of retail and traditional sales, so there is plenty of gray area to investigate.

# Retail Careers and Compensation

Many people associate retail sales with products such as clothing, housewares, beauty aids, and so on, where you may not spend a lot of time mastering the sales process. These positions are often entry level and pay a regular hourly rate.

Other retail positions pay a mix of bonuses and commissions along with a salary or hourly income. These jobs take a bit more mastery and can turn into fruitful careers for people who find success.

Sales of cell phones, electronics, jewelry, high-end clothing or shoes, furniture, spas, and other big-ticket or commitment products typically have the most aggressive performance-based compensation plans. Although anyone in retail can improve his sales process, these are the types of positions this chapter speaks to.

Be sure you understand how you're paid as a salesperson.

Make sure you have a clear picture of how you are paid as a salesperson. The way you are paid should not influence what you're selling to your customers in a true needs-based sales transaction, but it is important to allow money to motivate you.

Even if you aren't paid on performance or if it is a small percentage of your overall earnings, being a good salesperson can lead to all kinds of advancement opportunities. Your success can lead you into retail management, other better-paying retail opportunities, or even a position with a traditional sales company.

# Prospecting

Although the majority of retail customers come into a store because of an advertisement or prior knowledge of an establishment, prospecting isn't totally absent from the world of retail.

## Circle of Influence

As with any sales position, salespeople can solicit their friends, family, and associates. Some will do it directly, while others will do it in an indirect fashion. Here's a direct example over the phone:

> "Hey, Uncle Leo! I just wanted to give you a call and let you know we've got a sale on watches today. Thirty percent off on most models."

And here's an indirect example, done in person:

> "Hey, Uncle Leo! It's been a while. Things are good; I've been working at Tommy's Jewelry for almost a year now. If you ever want to stop in and check out some watches or grab something for Aunt Jane, I'll take good care of you."

The direct approach involves combing through personal contacts and directly asking them to come in and make a purchase. The indirect approach doesn't ask for the immediate sale, but it puts your name out there in case your contact needs to purchase your particular product.

Some retail salespeople choose to do a bit of prospecting by way of referral.

## Retail Referrals

Any other prospecting involved with retail sales comes from a referral basis. Anyone working in a storefront establishment can simply wait for customers to come in so they can let the sales process begin. There is nothing wrong with that approach, and that's generally how the game is played.

However, there are two types of retail referrals you can use to bring in extra clientele. First, you can solicit your circle of influence for referrals as well as for their business. Second, you can look for referrals through clients either at the point of sale or further down the road if clients have their contact information.

# Rapport Building

Traditional salespeople usually have a fair amount of time to build rapport with their new clients. Sometimes it's a few minutes at the beginning of a meeting, and other times an entire meeting will be dedicated to getting to know each other.

In retail sales, you have about 30 seconds to build rapport with a customer.

In retail sales, you have from the time a customer makes eye contact to 30 seconds or so of pleasantries.

Here is what you've probably experienced in the past:

> (Smiling) "Hi, how are you today? My name is Jennifer. Is there anything I can help you find today?"

From that point on, it's all business. To build rapport in a retail environment, you have to go back to the basics.

## Appearance

More so than in any other form of sales, storefront salespeople have to make sure they're pleasant and look approachable. You should wear ironed clothes, be well groomed, have a bright (but not phony) smile—anything that would put people at ease at the point of initial contact.

## Approach

Rushing to meet a person the minute she walks in the door of your store can be off-putting to some potential customers.

In some retail environments, customers' stomachs sink when they open the door and a salesperson comes flying across the room. Most people want to get acclimated to your store and do a bit of browsing before they make a buying decision. The ones who want your help immediately will seek you out.

This can be difficult to manage in many retail environments, because often you are competing with your own co-workers the minute someone walks in the door. I doubt a single suggestion from this book could change the way an entire retail chain does business, but sales teams should do their best to rotate through walk-in business. I know some do, but it's also blatantly obvious when you walk into a store where they don't.

If you have the opportunity for a casual approach that doesn't require a sprint, you're already a step ahead. Watching walk-in customers for a bit will tell you some things about them if you are observant. You should be able to tell who is worried about price by the way she looks at or talks about products. You can see who is in a rush and who is probably just killing time with no serious intention of buying. Paying attention to these signs and patterns will help you when it comes time to uncover your customer's needs.

When it seems like a reasonable time for you to step in, keep it simple and somewhere between friendly and formal. Pay attention to what you've observed and open up to your customer.

## Example 1

A customer has walked into the store. She spends little time looking at anything but the prices.

> "Hi, my name's Jeff! If I can help you find anything, let me know. We've got a great selection of sale items in the back if you're curious."

This customer was obviously price shopping. Jeff used a key observation to direct her to a sale section while also not attaching himself to a client who was likely price shopping. It can be difficult to "sell" anyone into anything if her only concern is browsing for a deal.

## Example 2

A customer walks into the store and gets hung up in one section, looking at two comparable products.

> "Hi, my name's Jeff. Is there something I can tell you about either of these products?"

Another obvious clue, but Jeff pays a little more attention to the comparison shopper. She is weighing the features and benefits of two things, and as a salesperson, he should be able to help out.

As you've probably noticed, these two examples didn't blow anyone away with rapport. Considering there is such a limited time in the opening with a customer, there isn't much you can do other than appear professional and approach with care.

True rapport building in retail sales happens throughout the entire sales process.

# Needs Analysis

At first glance, retail sales doesn't seem to require a needs analysis. People come into a store knowing what they need to buy. Just like prospecting, you could certainly get by without this step, but an efficient and effective retail salesperson will set out to take this step.

In retail sales, people come in seeking a specific product. As you know, not everyone coming in looking for a product leaves the store with one in hand.

*Find a way to amplify your customer's need for what you're selling.*

To prevent this non-sale, you must seek out ways to amplify your customer's need for whatever you are selling. Many salespeople focus on the features and benefits of their product, but your goal is to speak to the ones that meet the needs you have reinforced.

If someone wants to buy a television, he goes into a store, looks at several models, and decides on his own what fits his needs best. He might choose to visit several stores until he makes a purchase. To increase the odds of making a sale, the television salesperson must get the specifics behind her customer's buying decision. You might be thinking, "It's just a TV; he wants a TV because he wants to watch television." This is certainly true, but watch how the example unfolds.

Ellen works in an electronics store. Gus comes in and begins examining a few different flat-screen televisions. After some pleasantries, here is how Ellen does her needs analysis.

**Ellen:** So what kind of television are you looking for?

**Gus:** I'm not sure yet.

**Ellen:** Are you replacing an old one, or is it for an additional room?

**Gus:** I've got one of those big old bulky sets, and I think it's finally time to upgrade.

**Ellen:** Is something wrong with the old set?

**Gus:** Not really. I guess I'd just like something newer.

**Ellen:** Well, a TV is a TV…

**Gus:** Wow! Aren't you supposed to be selling me a television?

**Ellen:** Sure, but it's a big investment. What do you want a new television to do for you?

**Gus:** Honestly, it's just a little embarrassing having people over to watch stuff on the old set. I've put away some money for it, and I'm sure I'd like the better quality anyway.

Ellen did her needs analysis is a very unique way. First, she tried to back him off the television so he would solidify his own need in a sort of reactionary way. Then, Ellen made him qualify why he's making the purchase, thus uncovering what his true needs are. Because she knows he wants it to impress his friends, she can direct him toward a large screen or something with all kinds of bells and whistles. Throughout the rest of the sales process, she can talk toward features that might impress his friends.

# Presentation and Solution

This step of the sales process is quite similar to that in a traditional sales position. Based on your customer's needs, you are going to present products that best fit what they are looking for. It might sound obvious, but it is crucial that you speak to their deepest need.

> Speak to your customer's deepest need.

In the example of Ellen and Gus, she's *not* going to say:

"Here's a TV because you need a TV."

Because Ellen knows of Gus's deeper needs, she'll say (in perhaps different words):

"Here's the biggest freakin' TV we have; now you can impress your friends."

Making the connection between the product and the customer's deeper need fires up the urgency of the purchase while giving you the tools to find the right product to match your customer with.

# Closing

Retail closings are also similar to traditional sales closings. If you uncover needs and provide a solution, it will often happen on its own. Still, you will have to ask for the business in most cases.

Many retail purchases happen on a somewhat impulsive basis. There may be a need, but there may not be a real sense of urgency. When closing a retail sale, you must capitalize on the customer's impulses and give her little room to back out.

I'm not speaking of high-pressure sales or cornering anyone into purchasing; I'm saying that closing brings up a fundamental difference between retail and traditional sales.

In traditional sales, you want to continuously ask for confirmation to pull out objections and allow people to say no as early as possible so that you can avoid a drawn-out process for nothing.

In retail sales, you're not going to want to ask for confirmation the entire time. You want to feed the customer's impulses and *not* have her spending time considering whether she agrees.

An assumptive close is the best way to close a retail sale.

This is why an assumptive close is, hands down, the top way to close a retail sale. I may not be telling you something terribly new, because many salespeople already subscribe to this method.

Here are the kinds of closing or confirmations you want to avoid in the case of retail sales:

"So what do you think?"

"Is this what you want?"

"Okay, would you like to purchase this?"

"Do you want to think it over?"

The customer knows the answers to these questions in her head, and she will tell you if any of them are an issue. Putting these questions out there lets the customer go back to a more analytical way of purchasing, which tends to favor a drawn-out process.

Here is what an assumptive close sounds like. We'll return to Ellen and Gus in the electronics store.

**Ellen:** So, this television has one of the biggest screens available, and these features you've been playing with for the past 10 minutes really make up what is one of the most impressive televisions available.

**Gus:** I know. This is great, and the picture is amazing.

**Ellen:** Okay, are you going to finance this or pay cash or charge?

**Gus:** This one is a little out of my budget. Would a size down save me a lot?

**Ellen:** Yes, the 56-inch is on sale for $1,899.

**Gus:** Okay, that's a lot better. And it has the same features?

**Ellen:** It sure does, and we have it in stock! I'll have one of the warehouse guys bring it around front.

Ellen used a perfect example of an assumptive close twice in this example. First, she didn't ask him whether it was what he wanted; she closed as if she assumed he was going to buy and she needed to know how he would pay.

Gus didn't have a chance to say yes or no, but he was still able to voice his opinion over price. Ellen offered the new solution and went assumptive again by saying the warehouse would bring the television around.

# Retail Sales Positions

Because the world of retail sales encompasses so many different industries, it's worth looking at a few specific sales positions. The sales cycle within retail sales varies less than it does in other forms of sales, but there are some slight nuances associated with certain industries. Just remember that you can take away information across industries and even between retail, outside, and inside sales.

## Cell-Phone Sales

This is a relatively new type of sales position—that is, within the last couple of decades.

### Pros

Cell-phone salespeople have the highest average income for any kind of retail sales position. Opportunities to move up or around are high if your performance is substantial. While many retail sales positions are stepping stones, you can certainly make a career here based on mobility and income. Because wireless carriers operate on a national level, it can be easy to move around the country based on your personal needs and desires.

Wireless companies usually spend a fair amount of time and money on training. If you take advantage of this, it can help lead you to success while priming you with the tools for a move into another industry if you see fit.

### Cons

As with most retail jobs, your hours are dictated by the consumer. This requires evening and weekend work as a major part of your schedule.

Along with the higher income comes higher expectations. Although some retail positions pay mostly hourly or expect you to simply show up and facilitate the customer's purchase, cell sales managers will stay right on top of your numbers.

There is room for prospecting to some extent, but you can be at the mercy of your store's location or advertising. This is true for all retail, but it creates a bit of a challenge because your pay and employment are based on production.

### What Works

Cell-phone sales can be a great place to start, grow, or live out your sales career. Because the retail hours can cause people to burn out a bit more quickly than in other sales positions, be sure to have a well-defined plan for your future. If your plan is to move into management, post good numbers and play your cards right with the company brass. If you're using the position as a stepping stone, keep your numbers up and create some financial security so you can weather a future transition.

It seems that every other day, a new cell phone or service is available to the consumer. Be extremely educated on your own products as well as those of your competition. Know your products' strengths and weaknesses so you know how to match them up with the competition. Knowing product features in and out will create a better affinity between you and the consumer. Regardless of her needs, a potential customer will feel most comfortable with a salesperson who can quickly provide information and answers.

## Jewelry

This type of sales position has been around for many, many years and is likely to be around for years to come.

### Pros

The quality-of-life factor for most people working in jewelry sales is much higher than that of many other sales positions. Jewelry is a luxury item that people purchase for positive reasons. Salespeople are working with the soon-to-be-engaged or -married, couples of all kinds, and people simply looking to treat themselves or their loved ones to something nice with expendable income—as opposed to people making purchases out of necessity that are not necessarily a pleasant transaction.

Pay is somewhat driven by performance, so making a substantial amount of money for a retail position is quite possible. There is a bit more stability in this sales position compared to cell-phone sales or other traditional sales positions.

## Cons

Selling is involved, but much of what you do in this position is facilitation. Sales volume can be especially low at times and fluctuates with the seasons. This can affect your income level, and boredom levels can be tedious for the typical sales go-getter.

Jewelry salespeople deal with far more browsers than salespeople in any other sales position. It takes special skill as well as dumb luck to end up working with an active buyer.

## What Works

This is a position of facilitation, so the most important part of your job is making the customer feel at ease. Be presentable and helpful and do your best to keep customers engaged in your products.

If you want to make this into a long-term position, don't be afraid to do a bit of passive prospecting within your circle of influence. Be the salesperson your friends and family go to for their jewelry needs. Embrace the position and be their go-to person. Not only will you get their business, but you also stand to get some referrals, even if they haven't made a purchase from you themselves.

# Electronics

Another retail sales industry that is likely to be around for the long haul.

## Pros

Similar to jewelry sales, people making big-ticket electronics purchases are usually doing so out of pleasure as opposed to necessity. People enjoy getting caught up in the bells and whistles of televisions, computers, sound systems, and other fun items.

Most people who are drawn to this kind of a sales position already have an appreciation for technology, so it can be enjoyable to work with products you have an interest in. There is some incentive pay, but jobs in electronic sales usually have a more regular pay schedule and are a little less cutthroat in terms of sales numbers.

This is one of the best entry-level sales positions, especially for younger people looking to get their feet wet in sales in an industry to which they are typically drawn. They're able to work on their interpersonal skills without the high-intensity sales atmosphere.

## Cons

Income levels can be somewhat limiting unless you're working with extremely high-end products or full-service installations. Sales can vary greatly with the seasons, and some companies hire and fire based on the time of year and an easily replenished workforce.

The consumer knowledge gap can make the sales process more tedious than most. With the ever-changing world of technology, some consumers have difficulty grasping product function. This can turn the sales process into Electronics 101, which may not be what you've signed up for.

## What Works

Typically, it can be difficult to generate a sustainable income working in electronic sales unless you've mastered the process and sit at the top of your sales force. This can be a great place to learn about the sales process while making a bit more money than a usual retail or entry-level office position.

Unlike other sales positions, a move into electronics management can lead to even more volatility in your employment, as managers are usually the first to deal with the brunt of bad sales numbers or poor economic conditions. It may be best to plan on moving to a more typical sales position when you've run your course.

Commissions can vary from store to store and product to product, but the one constant is the profitability of selling warrantees. Unlike the product you're selling in the store, this service is intangible and thus allows for better pay percentages. Your company does the math on how often they have to service or replace products and makes this sale into a major profit center for you and for their bottom line.

# Furniture and Bedding

Yet another retail sales industry that won't be going away anytime soon.

## Pros

Furniture and bedding retail sales offers some of the widest ranges of sales positions within a single industry. Some low-ticket stores pay little to no commission and look to their sales force to act as facilitators, while others can offer big-ticket items with the pay to match. This is an advantage because you can find employment in this sales industry both on an entry-level basis or further down the road. Also, it's easier to stay in the industry and move up to better-paying sales positions than in any other retail sales job.

The necessity of furniture and bedding leaves this position less affected by seasonal sales patterns and economic conditions.

Furniture sales tickets can vary widely based on people's buying intentions. Some may walk away with a single recliner or a small kitchen table, but it's also not unusual for someone to come in and completely refurnish a large portion of her home. Financing packages help the consumer to stretch his dollar while giving you the opportunity for a large sale.

## Cons

The necessity factor of furniture and bedding can take some of the fun out of retail that other leisure and luxury items may have.

Although you do not fall prey to the seasons, much of this industry is driven by sales events. This can keep you busy during some of the usual month sales events, but it can also leave you pretty bored on your average weekday.

There is less room for "selling" than in other retail positions because most of the product is there for people to test out and touch.

## What Works

Furniture sales can offer you a decent living if you're willing to put in the hours to catch active walk-in buyers. If you have success with a more entry-level company, it is possible to move on to a more high-end store with better pay and product.

Make your customers feel at ease. Similar to car sales, the general public isn't always excited to have a salesperson intercept them right at the door. Let your client get acclimated and then help her when it looks as if she has a few questions and is getting ready to buy.

## Appliances

No other big-ticket items are "must haves" the way appliances are.

### Pros

Sales can be very steady because of necessity and the wide range of products usually available to appliance salespeople.

Bundling items can be more of a natural process with appliance sales. In very few other industries does someone come in looking for a thousand-dollar item and come out with two or three. Your company knows the potential for these kinds of sales, and this is why they offer great financing and bundled discounts for washers, dryers, refrigerators, dishwashers, and so on.

Appliance sales have a relatively healthy balance of stability and pay. You have some control over your income, but your employment is not based on passing whims. Subject to seasonal and sales events, there still is a pretty regular flow of customers even on a random weekday.

### Cons

People usually come in for these products when a prior one has kicked the bucket. Unless they're setting up a new home, this sales process can often start off on a negative note.

Because reliability is the number-one factor for these kinds of sales, consumers tend to do a bit of legwork and research before making a purchase. This can lead to stubborn certainty from your potential client and can sometimes eliminate most of the sales process—for better or worse.

Consumers tend to come directly to you if there is any problem with their product after the sale. Even with warrantees offered by your company and manufacturers, customers will often look to you to solve their newfound frustration.

## What Works

Focus on reliability factors early on in the sales process. Because most customers are replacing an item, this is where you'll have your biggest in. On the less likely chance that they're stocking a new house or looking for a fancy upgrade, read your customer and wow him with the bells and whistles.

Get your customer talking. The more he reveals about his home and needs, the more product you may be able to match up with his needs. The customer may be coming in for a dishwasher but on the fence about a refrigerator. If you can stir that up in conversation, it's easier to get the additional sale with a little combo discount, rather than forcing it down the customer's throat.

Sell your customer warrantees. As with electronics sales, they pay you well, but more importantly, you're doing your customer a favor. No matter how good the product, things combining the use of water, electric, gas, and drainage can cause headaches for you and your customer.

# Action Plan

Retail salespeople can learn from any section of this book, but this is your dedicated chapter to master.

- ✓ Understand how you are compensated as a retail salesperson.
- ✓ Think about what forms of prospecting you can do to bring in more customers.
- ✓ Observe and analyze customers before your opening.
- ✓ Make sure your appearance is suitable and that you approach customers in a welcoming way.
- ✓ Decide how you can uncover the needs of customers looking for the products you offer.
- ✓ Know the features and benefits of all your products so you can speak better to your customers' needs.
- ✓ Practice the assumptive close!

# Chapter 13

# Your 90-Day Plan

- Pre-90 Days
- Weeks 1 through 12
- Action Plan

Now it's time to streamline what you've learned into a 90-day plan. Although this book handled much of the material in a linear fashion, it's important to come up with a personalized plan of action. This action plan follows a pretty basic format that should be familiar to anyone in outside sales with a medium to long sales process. No matter what your sales process or industry is, follow this model and make the changes you see fit. This plan also starts off following a new hire. If you've been employed for some time, the slight changes and omissions you can make should be obvious.

Ninety days works out to about 12 work weeks, so I'll break this down on a week-to-week basis. Some of the content may become repetitive, but that's part of the point. Keeping your pipeline filled and processing sales will bring you success and stability.

# Pre-90 Days

Don't forget to have a financial cushion to get you through the lean period at the beginning of your sales career.

Before the official countdown, there are some obvious variables you cannot account for. First, you have to go through the hiring process. After that is out of the way, I'm not counting any formalized full-time training. As stated in earlier chapters, full-time training can range anywhere from a few days to several weeks or more. Week 1 starts your first day out of the gate as an official and functioning salesperson. Remember to have your finances in order or a secondary form of income ready to help you through your initial ramp-up phase.

# Week 1

Week 1 is about settling in and getting to know your co-workers.

Week 1 is all about getting settled in and comfortable with your surroundings, workload, and specific sales responsibilities. Your managers likely will have introductions and meetings scheduled throughout the week. Pay close attention in these meetings and get to know your fellow co-workers.

Set up your workspace as you see fit and be sure to move in some personal effects. Giving a sense of stability to yourself and your team is worth the small effort.

Sit down with your managers and get a well-defined picture of your territory, existing accounts, and any limitations you should be aware of within your prospecting role. Different companies divide up territory and leads in different ways, so be sure you know who you can and cannot go after.

If you walk into servicing some existing accounts, get the rap on the person who used to handle them, regardless of whether he is still with the company. This will help you get an idea of what the client may have been used to and will help you put out any fires before they spread.

Talk to any and all salespeople who are willing to give you pieces of advice. The veterans will be glad to share ideas if you take a genuine interest. There will also be naysayers. Although it is always best to surround yourself with the positive and successful salespeople, get a feel for what the disgruntled employees are frustrated with, too. Most areas of discontent will be excuses for their shortcomings, but you may learn a bit about the bumps you can expect in the road.

Take each and every piece of marketing material you have at your disposal and become a master of its content. If you're going to use any of these pieces as sales tools, you need to know them inside and out.

> Learn the contents of available marketing materials inside and out.

If your sales process has you in contact with clientele on a frequent basis, contact your existing accounts and let them know you'll be handling their accounts from here forward. You don't have to let on about your newness to the company, but you should set up some meetings as soon as possible to meet them and/or continue servicing their accounts.

Devise a plan of attack for prospecting, as that's what Week 2 will be all about!

# Week 2

Settled into your new sales position with a better sense of your position and your company's infrastructure, it's time to hit the ground running.

You might already be meeting with existing clientele this week. Based on client history and value, determine whether you should make your introduction on your own or with a sales manager. Sales managers can be your biggest advocates in a seamless transition to running the account.

Begin prospecting in Week 2.

Prospecting starts now. Some companies will provide you with leads, while others will plop down a phone book (or a computer) and tell you to get on the phones! Work with your scripts and tailor them to your own comfort level.

If you have a geographically designated territory, consider pounding the pavement and making introductions. Come in relatively unarmed, save for a few business cards. Let prospective clients know that you look forward to working with them in the future and that you will be calling on them to set up an initial sales meeting. Some may do it on the spot; others will tell you not to bother. Keep charging forward.

Go along on your co-workers' sales calls when you have a chance. It's a great way to learn this new position.

Continue to absorb any training being offered by your management. You will want people to come along on your appointments from time to time, but also find a few people who are willing to take you on theirs. Clients of all kinds are used to seeing salespeople training in the field. Be a fly on the wall or chime in if your co-worker would like your opinion. You can learn a lot by watching.

By the end of the week, you should have introduced yourself to existing clients as well as to some portion of your new business territory, giving you work to do in Week 3.

# Week 3

By Week 3 you should be conducting sales calls.

In Week 3, you should be conducting sales calls with a portion of your existing clientele. Prepare to uncover your clients' needs in these meetings and solidify that your product or service can meet those needs. Again, some of these meetings could benefit from the presence of a manager.

Your prospecting from last week should have yielded some introductory meetings with leads. You might find that these meetings are better conducted on your own in a low-pressure, rapport-building situation. However, if you plan to bring in a sales manager at a later date, it will help to allow him to build rapport as well. Pick and choose carefully how you run your initial introductory meetings. Fight off any urges—whether personal or brought on by your new lead—to launch into a presentation of any kind. If the meeting is going to go further, make sure it is about the customer and her needs.

If you plan to conduct business or seek out referrals within your own personal sphere of influence, right around Week 3 is when you may be comfortable enough to have those conversations.

Continue your prospecting to keep the pipeline full. Follow up with people you missed and take good notes about all of your experiences attempting to contact or set appointments with new clientele.

# Week 4

In Week 4, you should be making presentations and even closing with people in your existing customer database. You should follow up new-business leads that you met last week with sales calls to uncover the clients' needs. Some presentations or closings with new business may even sneak into this week.

*By Week 4 you may be starting to close some sales.*

Thirty days into your 90-day plan, you should have enough personal experience to know what some of the more common objections in your industry are. Talk to your managers and other top reps to strategize ways to overcome these familiar objections. Find a consistent response that you believe in and that makes you most comfortable upon delivery.

Depending on how large your customer base is, you should have touched a majority of your leads at this point.

# Week 5

In Week 5, you should be posting pretty competitive numbers with your group, depending on your mix of new and returning business. New-business accounts should be closing, and your existing-revenue accounts should be operating full steam ahead.

Week 5 starts a new plan of attack.

Because you have worked through a majority of your leads at this point, it's important to prioritize and form a new plan of attack. Compose a letter for leads that you feel have the most potential. State your desire to have a meeting and let them know you intend to contact them soon.

By the end of the month, you should be comfortable going on calls by yourself, for the most part. You might have a few large or complicated accounts that you need help with, but you should have the basic process down pat. Consider a few final ride-alongs with a manager or a veteran rep. Ask that person to be more of a fly on the wall but to give you his full opinion on your sales process. Take his advice to heart and work on your weaknesses.

# Week 6

Around Week 6, you should start focusing on getting referrals.

You've closed a fair amount of business this point, so it's important to start focusing more on referrals from your budding client base. Ask for referrals after business has closed or when your product or service is being delivered.

Even though your initial leads have been picked over, rotate back through in an attempt to set a meeting with those you have not been able to reach. Some of your prospects from Week 2 have not been contacted in at least a month. Even if you get some no answers to thin out your lead database, you're still making progress.

As a newer salesperson, you might have gone for some soft closes or left a few presentations open with clients. It's important to get back in touch with these clients and ask for their business. As the weeks go by, you will learn to schedule and close within a very specific timeframe. Use Week 6 to play a bit of catch-up, especially with the existing clients to whom you presented three weeks ago.

# Week 7

In Week 5, you sent out a mailer to a large chunk of your top leads. Follow up with a phone call or drop by in an attempt to make an appointment.

Around this halfway point, it's important to do a self-assessment of your personal strengths and weaknesses. You're experienced enough to know where you need help, but you're still new enough to ask for help from your available resources.

Take advantage of your managers at this halfway point and let them know that it is your goal to be one of the top salespeople within the next month and a half. Any points of learning you've missed in a self-assessment likely can be pointed out by a manager or even a helpful sales veteran.

Make sure none of your new-business recommendations has stayed open for too long. Get in touch with these clients and ask for their business. Tighten up your timeframe for closing on new accounts, the same way you have with your existing clientele.

> In Week 7, follow up with the leads you contacted by mail in Week 5. Week 7 is also a good time to do an assessment of your strengths and weaknesses as a salesperson.

# Week 8

Sixty days into your 90-day process, you should be feeling pretty comfortable with your new co-workers. If you have any interest in becoming a manager or you would just like to be a team player, start taking a more active role in training, meetings, and any other group functions.

Believe it or not, you might find that you're not the newest kid on the block just two months into your sales career. Help along the new sales reps while keeping an open mind so you can continue to learn, even from the newer blood.

Two weeks earlier, you had an extra focus on asking for referrals. Make sure you have contacted all of your new referrals from your initial sales and get them into your pipeline. Set up initial meetings and have the person giving you the referral make personal introductions when she can.

You should always be prospecting. As with every previous week, work on your cold calling and continue to reach out to each and every potential client you can.

> In Week 8, focus on taking an active role in team-related activities and goals.

# Week 9

In Week 9, your business should be working itself into a perfect balance that you should be able to maintain for as long as you so choose.

In Week 9, make service calls to any clients with whom you haven't spoken since your earlier closes with them.

Make service calls to any of your clients you have not spoken to since your closes earlier in the process. These service calls should become a continual part of your sales process from here on out. Create a scheduling system that will keep you on top of your contact activities. This is especially important if you are working in an industry with a less frequent sales cycle.

Two months into this process, you will have experienced a full sales cycle. You will have clients you prospected for on your own. After several sales meetings, you'll have a signed contract to turn in for processing. Your first commissions will be coming through, and you will be placing your first follow-up service calls.

Pay close attention to the length of this sales process. It can vary greatly from industry to industry. Having a good sense of this will help you pace your business activity and have a better understanding of your personal finances with regard to your income.

Knowing how long the cycle takes from start to finish can often be a great motivating factor if you lose your appetite for prospecting.

"I don't want to make these calls, but I know I have to. It takes an average of six weeks from the time I make these calls until there is money in my pocket."

These reminders can help with your self-discipline and keep you on the phones. As always, spend some time cold calling this week.

# Week 10

By Week 10 your commissions should be coming in, so it's time to think about giving up the secondary job you worked while waiting for your sales income to start rolling in, if you went that route.

One month after your first serious week of reported sales, you should begin to feel the full effects of your commissioned income. This is a great time to get a good grasp on your personal budgeting. Any secondary job you have been working in the interim should be wrapping up by this point. You may enjoy the extra income, but you're a full-fledged salesperson now. Financially speaking, your time is better spent prospecting and meeting with clients.

Sit down and review your personal goals. Now that you have a better concept of your earnings, you can make plans to reap the benefits. Review your business goals as well. Consider how much money you have earned and see what kind of room you have for even further growth and business. Let the money be your motivator!

With a bit of financial comfort and confidence in your new position, this is the time to consider joining community groups and taking part in social events of all kinds. Make new contacts and expand your book of business while doing something to enrich your life.

*At this point, you should start taking part in social events and community groups.*

Start running many of your meetings as a coffee or meal with your potential clients. Invest in your sales career by treating some of your clients to something that will help build immediate rapport. Keep track of these expenditures and make sure you're working within the legal realm of your sales position.

# Week 11

Week 11 should be when you solidify a typical daily and weekly schedule. Set aside time each day for prospecting new leads, calling on referrals, servicing existing clients, and holding sales meetings. Make sure the sales meetings are balanced as well. You should have a good mix of introductory meetings scheduled along with needs-discovery, presentations, recommendations, and closes.

*Solidify your daily and weekly schedule in Week 11.*

If you try to turn this process into a monthly schedule, you may create a ripple effect in your sales process. Prospecting one week, holding initial sales meetings the next, presenting one week later, and then bunching your closing into a final week will disrupt your process.

Take a look at your current workload and figure out what your capacity may be. Forecasting your capacity will help you learn how to prioritize your duties and where you can trim the fat. If your industry allows for it, this is a prime time to start thinking about the pros and cons of hiring an assistant.

Some of your referral business will come together at this time. Recognize and appreciate the difference between conducting business via cold calls and finding clients through referrals and introductions. You will quickly learn why referrals, introductions, and warm leads are so valuable.

# Week 12

By Week 12, you *can* be one of the top sales reps on your team.

There is nothing preventing you from being one of the top sales reps in your office by Week 12. Some may have more revenue accounts or be in different places than you, but you will have defined yourself as a key player on your team.

Only three months into the process, your managers may put the idea in your head about whether you've ever considered getting into management. Maybe you have, maybe you haven't, but at least you know you've made a name for yourself.

Three months of hard work and disciplined prospecting will help you find a great deal of success in sales. Take a look at where you are now. Is this something you could do for several more years? Ten more years?

From here on out, your weekly sales process should look similar and follow your defined schedule. In time, your position may be mostly consumed with servicing and selling to existing clientele. Always leave a little time for prospecting, because you never know when you may lose any number of your accounts.

# Action Plan

Use the entirety of Chapter 13 along with this checklist to put yourself on track for 90 days to success in sales. Make sure you tailor it to your specific industry and sales process.

### Week 1:

✓ Settle in.

✓ Define your territory.

✓ Contact your inherited accounts.

**Week 2:**

✓ Begin prospecting.

✓ Meet with your inherited accounts.

✓ Wrap up your in-house training.

**Week 3:**

✓ Present to your inherited accounts.

✓ Conduct initial meetings with new clientele.

✓ Continue prospecting and contact your circle of influence.

**Week 4:**

✓ Close on inherited accounts.

✓ Uncover the needs of new clientele.

✓ Work on your objection handling.

**Week 5:**

✓ Sales closed should be competitive.

✓ Compose a letter for new prospects.

✓ Go on final ride-alongs for assessment.

**Week 6:**

✓ Focus on obtaining referrals from recent business.

✓ Start over and rework your leads.

✓ Close any straggling recommendations to existing clients.

**Week 7:**

✓ Contact the businesses you mailed to in Week 5.

✓ Assess your strengths and weaknesses.

✓ Close any straggling recommendations to new clients.

**Week 8:**

✓ Take an active role within your sales team.

✓ Call on referrals.

✓ Continue to cold call.

**Week 9:**

✓ Place follow-up calls to clients with whom you have conducted business.

✓ Recognize the length of your complete sales cycle.

✓ Continue to prospect, open, and close business.

**Week 10:**

✓ Review your personal goals and finances.

✓ Participate in the community.

✓ Conduct some business over coffee or meals.

**Week 11:**

✓ Build your daily and weekly schedule.

✓ Forecast your capacity.

✓ Close and express appreciation for referral business.

**Week 12:**

✓ Consider management and your future.

✓ Get into a sustainable sales rhythm.

✓ Always prospect and ask for referrals.

# Chapter 14

# Beyond 90 Days

- Extended Planning
- Long-Term Client Management
- Continued Education
- Sales Assistants
- Career Changes
- Retirement
- Action Plan

In 90 days, it is very possible to start or turn around a sales career if you exercise discipline and good planning. After your initial 90 days, there are many things that go into continued success in sales. Anyone who has been in sales for some time knows what "flash in the pan" salespeople are. They come in and have a great amount of initial success. Some people write it off as beginner's luck, and others understand how a short-lived sales career works.

In a new and uncharted job, people tend to give it their all and make sure they cover all the bases. They put in the hours and do the extra work because they're never sure what's enough. This kind of work ethic can pay off, but often it leads to a point of complacency.

The people who put in all the initial effort begin to learn the ropes. They know what's needed and not needed, and they learn where they can get away with cutting corners. Their newfound success gives them a bit of financial stability, so they're operating with an even higher comfort level.

As these employees let off on the gas, things don't look quite as rosy. Numbers begin to dip, and the highly charged work ethic begins to normalize.

The salespeople who were used to accolades for a job well done as well as swollen paychecks see these perks fall by the wayside. This is when some people decide to revisit their efforts, while others crash and burn from the impending failure.

You can prevent this kind of flash-in-the-pan experience by planning to advance your career successfully well beyond 90 days.

## Extended Planning

Create a clear roadmap to move successfully beyond 90 days in the sales industry.

The best way to move successfully beyond 90 days is by creating a clear roadmap. You can base extended plans on goals and benchmarks that seem in line with your initial sales experience. You must expect that there will be some leveling out, but that is why it's good to have some time under your belt so you can build realistic goals.

Your company will likely provide you with annual goals, so it's important to make sure they coincide with your personal intentions. It's probably not a good idea to plan to do *less* than the company expects of you, but it's also important to be realistic about your abilities and threshold.

In prior chapters we've talked about goal setting and having daily plans. For long-term success in sales, it's crucial to develop a plan that encompasses all aspects of success in sales. Once you develop this plan, it's important to stick with it for as long as possible. You may be tempted to make changes because of redundancy or simply because you feel you're in a rut, but it's important that you do not waver. Making changes to your plan on a whim will certainly send you off course.

> Develop a plan that encompasses all aspects of success in sales.

When you're up and running to your capacity and comfort level, you can develop your extended planning. The phrase "extended planning" might sound like a grand overall view of your career, but it's really based on your day-to-day activity.

Your daily (or weekly, depending on your sales process) plan must encompass all aspects of the sales process. You must spend time prospecting. You must spend time meeting with new clients. You must build proposals, and you must service your existing accounts.

Waiting to build this plan is important because you will not have a good sense of these proportions until you've spent some time in the field. It might turn out that you have to spend a major part of your time servicing your existing accounts. On the other hand, your sales process may be infrequent, so there is little to no servicing of past clients.

A car salesman usually won't want to call the guy to whom he just sold a car on a weekly basis. However, someone who set up a new network for a small business may need to do so for some time.

When you have a fair assessment of your sales position, setting up a very regular system will allow you to ride your success for as long as you wish. Here are some examples of how people set up a very regular schedule based on their position's needs.

## Example 1

Kate sells newspaper and online ads for a local publication in her hometown. She has been working for almost a year and has a good sense of what it will take to have continued success.

**8–9 a.m.** Build spec ads and communicate with the art department and production for new and existing client ads.

**9–10 a.m.** Contact existing clients for ad changes and any billing issues.

**10–11 a.m.** Prospect for new business through leads, referrals, and cold calling.

**11–12 p.m.** Have an in-house meeting with a new or existing client.

**12–1 p.m.** Lunch.

**1–3 p.m.** Hold appointments outside the office at clients' convenience.

**3–4 p.m.** Prospect and cold call on foot or by car in proximity to appointments. Stop in on inactive clients.

**4–5 p.m.** Turn in new contracts and ad layouts.

Kate's career has leveled out, but she still wants to grow her business at a steady pace. As opposed to the beginning of her career, when she was cold calling most of the time, she now has clients that need servicing. That being said, she still manages to spend two hours on prospecting in various ways. Her day is sandwiched with paperwork to make sure she doesn't leave any loose ends at the beginning or end of the day.

While her day can be left to the whims of her clients and their scheduling abilities, she tries to follow this format whenever possible.

She may be tempted to cut back on the prospecting when she's busy with existing clients, but she'll soon lose business through unreplaced attrition.

Kate may also try to improve her bottom line by prospecting more and cutting into the time she services accounts. This lack of customer service would lead to disgruntled clients and ad errors.

## Example 2

Kevin works in pharmaceutical sales. He is up and running at a good pace but wants to avoid being another flash-in-the-pan salesperson. With the longer sales process, Kevin prefers to build his sustainable plan on a weekly basis.

**Monday:** Office day. Sales meetings in the morning and paperwork in the afternoon. The schedule for the week is polished and confirmed.

**Tuesday:** Active-doctor visits. Drop by with script pads, samples, and marketing materials and fill any other needs with existing clientele.

**Wednesday:** Prospecting. New and follow-up calls on cold leads and information drops with warmed leads.

**Thursday:** Seminars held or planned. This day is devoted to running or planning luncheons, dinners, workshops, or seminars.

**Friday:** Mornings spent meeting with new clients as scheduled. Afternoons spent meeting with top clientele as needed. Some Friday afternoons left for personal time if weekend appointments are going to be held.

Although Kevin has a looser schedule than our first example, it still focuses on portioning out all aspects of his sales process. He's meeting with existing clients while prospecting and working with new potential clientele.

Kevin starts his week getting all the office work out of the way so he can focus the rest of his week on clients of all kinds. It's important for him to reserve Friday afternoons for himself, as he may have to take weekend appointments from time to time.

# Long-Term Client Management

The most valuable clients you have are the ones you are doing business with. It's not the big fish you've been courting for months or the countless other prospects you have. Prospecting is the most important part of the sales process, but that's because you are trying to acquire long-term clients.

> Your most valuable clients are the ones you're doing business with.

Managing your relationship with a client can be very similar to managing your relationships with anyone else. You need to give clients attention but not smother them. You have to be reliable, but you have to keep their attention with ideas for growth and exceptional service they're not used to.

*Your existing clients' needs always come first.* Although prospecting is important, your existing customers' needs come first. Because there are no set expectations with prospecting, you can do it at anytime and in any way. Existing clients need you when they need you. You have to work with their schedule, and you have to deliver what they're looking for.

Beyond handling your clientele on a business level, it's likely you will grow to know each other on a personal level to some extent. Nurturing this relationship will be fruitful on both a personal and a business level.

It's important to first identify the clients that you see yourself doing business with for years. This could be based on a variety of factors, including the business you're in. These clients aren't always the biggest spenders from transaction to transaction, but their value over the years will add up.

Long-term clients must have an evident longevity with their current business or status. A business owner who is relatively young and driven to keep business booming for decades is an excellent example—as opposed to someone closer to retirement, who may close down or sell off the business. Even if they're not older, some unmotivated business owners may be difficult to build long-lasting relationships with.

*Potential long-term clients sometimes need a little extra attention.* After you've identified these clients, you must have a plan of action to nurture the relationships. All of your clients deserve and have paid for your professional abilities with product and services. Clients with long-term potential may just need a little extra attention.

The most basic part of your plan is great customer service. Again, no one deserves lesser customer service than anyone else, but it's important to shoot for a flawless track record over the long term with these specific customers. Deliver as promised. Be prompt and on time for all appointments. Answer their questions to the best of your abilities and get help on those you cannot answer. If a mistake is made, do everything in your power to correct and compensate for the situation.

After you keep the basic customer service intact, start to consider some more long-term rapport-building strategies.

Most customers have to provide their birth date somewhere on the contract if credit is a part of your transaction. If not, there's nothing wrong with asking for it. Stay on top of these dates and send off a card or a simple gift if it's not against your industry's code of ethics. Even if it's a gift card for coffee or gas, it's still more than most of their sales reps are doing.

Some companies have customer-appreciation events. Do your best to have your top clients be involved. It will allow them to further connect with you and your associates on a personal level. If your company doesn't do anything like this, consider holding an event of your own. Maybe it's just a barbecue or cocktail party. An even simpler and more affordable idea is a joint fundraising event. I once worked with a small group of my clients to refurbish a home for the community out of our own pockets. It was a great way to give back, and it built stronger rapport than any other event I could have put together.

If you become full-blown friends with your client, that's great. Just be sure to not ruin either relationship with too many crossed wires. Your friend someday may have to stop doing business with you. Your business client may someday get on your nerves as a friend. Keep it balanced and separate, and you should be fine.

# Continued Education

If you're picking up this book in the first place, you already understand the value of education. People have been in your shoes before, and they want to share with you. Others can keep you informed in ways your position or company doesn't bother with. Higher education will give you new tools as well as resume fodder.

## Sales Books and Seminars

While I have told you throughout this book that there aren't any tricks to sales or quick ways to make a million, there is still some value in listening to other people's messages of success in sales.

Some of these people will use a few trendy ideas to sell their books or seminars. These ideas may be gimmicks to promote their own sales numbers, but it's likely that the experiences can lend some value to your overall education.

Often these books and seminars are meant to motivate and move you to action. These tools can be effective in sales due to the amount of passion required to be successful in sales. Also, the people typically drawn to sales tend to have personalities that are easily motivated. They're motivated by money and accolades, but the passionate stories of struggle and success that others can share usually have a similar effect.

## Product Education

*Always take full advantage of your company's product-education offerings.*

After your initial training, most companies will offer continual learning and education on your product, service, and industry. Take full advantage of these offerings, even in the latest parts of your career.

I recall being in a sales position that offered weekly training due to the wide range of products we sold. Some of the veterans would opt out of these meetings, and upon later conversation, we would uncover that there was something totally new they'd never learned about. There's no need to be too proud to accept extra help through education.

Outside of your company's offerings, it's a good idea to seek out other educational venues for your line of work. Subscribe to industry magazines or newsletters. Research your own products through the eyes of a third party. Knowing more about your product than your own company will tell you will pay off exponentially. Hearing about the good, the bad, and the competition can only make you a stronger sales rep.

If your industry offers any kind of certifications, seek them out. Regardless of whether they're technical or financial certifications, not only will you learn more, but you will also give your clients more of a reason to choose to do business with you.

## Higher Education

Many large companies will pay for some or all of your education. Whether you need the education to better your career or yourself, take full advantage. I once worked in a sales position for a company that reimbursed any accredited education 100 percent. Totally unrelated to my career, I took a psychology class and one on media.

The most obvious educational goal to seek out while working is either your undergraduate degree or your MBA. However, most professionals and educators agree—and often require—that experience in the business world comes before the pursuit of an MBA.

If you are looking to eventually move into management, an MBA is one of the best steps you can take to move into this position with success. You may not need it for some lower-level management positions, but the knowledge you acquire will be far more pertinent than what you recall from your undergrad education (in my humble opinion).

> To eventually move into a management position, an MBA is a valuable tool.

MBA programs understand that they need to cater to business professionals. It's becoming far more commonplace for classes to be available in the evenings and online for people who are part of the regular workforce.

Take advantage of your company's education-reimbursement plan, even if it's not to get your MBA. If you have your undergraduate degree, why not get your master's in a topic of interest to you or one that might help with your business career?

Someone working in advertising sales could benefit from a master's degree in marketing. A salesperson with any kind of technology company could find a plethora of degrees that would help her further her career. Even if you don't go for something related to your career, enriching your life in any way will help prevent burnout and will likely teach you things that will come up somewhere down the road.

## Sales Assistants

One of the hardest things for business owners to do is delegate duties. Many prefer to have their hands on every aspect of the day-to-day grind. This can be one of the roadblocks business owners face in growing to new levels. If they cannot delegate and bring in enough employees to manage various duties, they can only grow to the level of their own personal limitations.

The same can be said for sales. Sales positions are very entrepreneurial, and you may come to a similar crossroads in your sales career. Taking on a sales assistant can lighten the burden of certain daily work aspects so that you can focus on money-making sales.

> A sales assistant can take on certain daily work tasks, freeing you up to focus on making sales.

Early in your career, you should calculate what your time is worth. After commissions and salary, what can you really earn hourly when going through the sales process? This will allow you to qualify the added expense of a sales assistant. If you're spending 20 hours a week doing paperwork and other jobs not directly related to the sales process, it may make sense for you to bring on an assistant.

Any task you can teach can easily be handed over to a qualified person. If you're comfortable with your assistant's customer service skills, he can even set appointments and do some level of customer follow-up.

The goal behind hiring a sales assistant is to ultimately bring in more money. If you bring in a part-time sales assistant who costs you $300 per week, you must be able to use your freed-up time to make more than $300 in additional funds.

Depending on the flexibility of your company and industry, you may even be able to bring in your own salespeople to help with those duties. This is quite common in real estate and even financial planning.

## Career Changes

Most people in the current workforce will have almost a dozen jobs over the course of their career. This isn't any different in sales, and quite frankly, it could be even more commonplace.

It's important for you to determine early on whether your job is going to blossom into a career or whether it's going to lead you to other opportunities outside your company.

Never think of your current job as *only* a stepping stone.

If it's your plan to move on after some time, it's important not to get too caught up in the fact that your current job may be just a stepping stone. This can breed a bad attitude toward work and ultimately lead you to fail at your current job and miss the opportunity to move on to another.

However, consciously deciding that you will be moving on can help motivate you if you're at a less-than-rewarding job. You may get your start in sales with a retail position with tough hours. As long as you know your success will lead you to a more desirable job, you should be motivated.

When you're using a sales job as a stepping stone, it's very important to overachieve. The whole purpose of taking a starter job is so that you can have references and experiences that will lead you to a real career. Knowing this, it's important to have a good relationship with your management and co-workers. This is another reason not to get too caught up with the "stepping stone" concept. If you spend the whole time acting as if you're better than everyone you're working with, you'll have a hard time getting references, let alone finding success.

Be sure to document your initial career successes. Salesperson of the week/month/year accolades can help, but also consider holding onto your pay stubs and tax returns. This can help you qualify the salary or income target you're looking for in your next job. It's also a very unorthodox way of proving your success with a prior company. I'm not saying you should staple these to your resume, but don't be afraid to let your potential employers know they're available upon request. Just be sure the information you are sharing isn't proprietary to your previous employer.

Not everyone who spends time in sales plans on spending his entire career in sales. Sometimes the product or service you are selling can lead you to other non-sales opportunities.

Much of my personal experience in sales was through marketing and advertising sales. This experience made me such an expert on the topic that I was able to turn it into a consulting career.

The non-sales positions you find may even be within the company you're already working for. This can help you make a seamless transition out of sales if that is your wish. Your continued education through your sales career will make it even easier for you to find outside employment.

With the entrepreneurial spirit that most salespeople embody, becoming a small-business owner is also a sensible move for some salespeople. You may stay in your own industry, or you might just use your sales knowledge to grow a different style of business.

As a business owner, you will always be a part of a sales process, so prior experience in sales is debatably more important than experience in the industry into which you're moving. The work ethic that matches up with sales lends itself to success in business.

Understanding that work isn't always 40 hours per week and a 9-to-5 schedule will get you ready for the grind that is owning a business. Your experience with fluctuating income will prepare you for a similar experience as a business owner. Just remember to have enough money to live, as well as money to invest in your startup or business purchase. And most important, don't forget to pick up a copy of *90 Days to Success Marketing and Advertising your Small Business* by yours truly....

# Retirement

The ultimate goal and end game to any career is the way you wrap it up in the end. People's career aspirations may be to make a difference in other people's lives and leave a mark for future generations, but it's exceedingly important to plan well for your own retirement.

Retirement can come at any age, depending on how well you plan and how you want to live out your life. Always take advantage of your company's retirement plan–matching opportunities and consider any stock payout options if you feel the company you're working for is solvent and heading in the right direction.

It takes a lot of discipline to save, but it's a must for anyone who wants to retire at a reasonable age. In the uncertain political world, it may be best not to rely too heavily on Social Security. Set goals for saving for retirement each year. Remember that savings is one thing, and saving for retirement is another. There are many tax advantages to saving your money correctly for retirement.

One great thing about retiring out of a sales career is your ability to keep your foot in the door. Some companies will pay you for life from any money earned from an account you brought in. Others will let you stay on board part time to manage some of your top accounts. This passive income will lighten your savings burden and allow you to live out your retirement as you see fit.

# Action Plan

✓ Consider any extended plans you have for your career.

✓ Think about how you manage your long-term clients.

✓ Take part in continuing education.

✓ Consider the kinds of changes you plan on making in your career in the long term.

✓ Prepare for retirement.

# Chapter 15

# Thirty-Three A.S.T.

Now that you have completed the bulk of this book, there is one more chapter for your reading pleasure. Throughout this entire book, I have told you that the keys to sales are prospecting, uncovering needs, and providing solutions. I have also told you that there are no tricks to sales. This is still true. However, I would be doing you a disservice if I didn't share some of the unique ins and outs of sales that I have picked up over the years.

I shortened this chapter's title from "Thirty-Three Advanced Sales Techniques" to attempt to prevent the fly-by-night salespeople from skipping past all the meat and potatoes to pick up a few tricks to improve their sales game. These fun and somewhat anecdotal ideas may give you a few tricks—er, techniques—to keep up your sleeve.

1. **Dress for the occasion.** Don't walk in to visit a mechanic wearing your best three-piece suit, and don't show up for a meeting with an attorney wearing jeans and a polo shirt. It sounds simplistic and judgmental, but you will be judged on your appearance. It has nothing to do with class association or anything pretentious—this is just a way to put people at ease and make them feel as if they can better relate to you.

2. **Be interested in everything.** No matter what you see or what someone tells you, take an interest, and you will build rapport. Look around the waiting room or pay attention to the pictures and trinkets displayed on the wall. If your client starts out talking casually about a particular subject, it's because she has an interest in it. I'm not saying you have to completely pretend to enjoy the exact same things, but find an avenue through which you can relate.

3. **Always jot down some quick notes throughout your conversation.** Don't slow it down by writing a dissertation, but don't sit there with your arms folded, nodding the whole time. It needs to be clear to your customer that you are taking him very seriously. When a customer sees a salesperson sitting there without taking a note, he will feel as if you're not paying attention, and your proposal will be based on *your* needs, not his.

4. **Always let your client know that other people have felt the same way.** Chances are, most of your customers will have similar needs and concerns. Sharing makes them feel as if their concerns are real and that you or your company has dealt with them in the past. If you've heard it before, you should be able to deal with it very well. Think of how the opposite would make a client feel: "We've never seen that before, but I'm sure we'll figure something out!"

5. **Smile when you can.** It's another simple idea, but it will work wonders in making you come across as agreeable and easygoing. Sure, you're selling a serious product and your company sets the gold standard for tradition in your industry, but your client is doing business with you. He wants to work with someone he can get along with.

6. **Shake everyone's hand.** This should be an obvious one, but you'd be surprised how many people leave it out. Shake the hand of your contact as well as anyone else in her party. Make sure you do it when you meet and when you part. Make sure your handshake is firm, not limp but also not overbearing. No one will think twice about a normal handshake, but if you offer up a limp noodle or try to break your client's fingers, it will start things off on an awkward foot.

7. **Return your phone calls immediately.** People want immediate satisfaction and may be able to find it elsewhere. Don't put off returning the bad calls, because they only get worse with time. If you don't answer or return calls, your competition will. Screening phone calls does you no good. You might be nervous about getting caught off guard, but dealing with a customer promptly, whether she is happy or disgruntled, is always the best idea.

8. **Attend unorthodox networking events.** Formalized networking events are bloated with insurance salespeople and the same old faces trying to sell each other. Business cards will get shuffled around, and you'll start to see the same people there. Instead, head to a town hall meeting or a fundraiser. You'll learn more, enjoy yourself, and catch people off guard in a good way.

9. **Always ask people what they do before offering up your own spiel.** If you want people to take a genuine interest in you and what you're selling, you must learn about them first. When you attend social gatherings, don't be a wallflower. Go up and ask people about themselves. They'll be glad to brag or boast a bit and then generally reciprocate the line of questioning.

10. **Seek out business in trade when your company will allow.** Restaurants love to do business for gift certificates, and the fringe benefits and compensation can be a lot of fun. You usually cannot be commissioned for cash on trade, but if you did the work, your company may share in the trade value. This tactic can lend itself to somewhat of an easier sale, albeit with payment in an unorthodox fashion.

11. **Spend a few bucks on advertising.** Your competition and coworkers aren't doing it, and your employer may pick up some of the cost if you do it right. Depending on your industry, check out unique avenues such as church bulletin or sponsorship opportunities. Businesses advertise. As a salesperson, you are as close to holding a DBA as possible. Market and advertise for a bit of call-in business.

12. **Don't be a know-it-all.** Customers will trust you when you aren't afraid to ask others for advice. You'll service them better by not faking it, and they will be glad you're seeking out the best response by consulting others.

13. **Don't be an idiot.** Customers will not trust you when you have to ask someone else about every aspect of your own product or service. It's important to ask when you don't know, but when you don't know anything, no one will want to do business with you. Know your product and marketing materials inside out so that you can keep the calls for assists to a minimum.

14. **Don't sell your customer short based on your personal limiting beliefs.** Just because you can't afford to spend thousands of dollars on something doesn't mean that your customer can't. Time and time again, I have seen salespeople present very low-cost proposals because they were too scared or they thought people couldn't spend more—based on nothing more than their limiting beliefs. Look around your office. People are asking their clients to spend large amounts of money and having success in doing so.

15. **Always ask your customers whether they'd accept referrals from you.** Give them some if you can, but asking them first will often result in a returned favor. If you want to take it one step further, set up a list of preferred vendors. Get people from all different industries into your database so that you can refer out to other people looking for their product or service. Obviously, you should try to get your customers some business if it comes up, but this is also a way to get them to offer up referrals willingly and with gratitude.

16. **Share minimal prospecting stories with your managers.** Yes, you should have an open line of communication with your managers, but it shouldn't turn into an information feeding frenzy. They will ask you about each and every one until it's turned into a sale or a chance for them to tell you what you've done wrong. There's no benefit to sharing unless you need help. Always under-promise and under-report and then over-produce and over-deliver.

17. **Share relevant personal stories with your clients when the time and occasion is right.** So much of rapport building is about making clients feel as if they can relate to you. If you can relate to them through your past experiences, take the opportunity to let them know indirectly.

    **Client:** We just bought a place up on Lake Lawrence.

    **You:** Oh, I love Lake Lawrence! I spent a summer working at Bill's Bar back in college.

18. **Don't bog down your clients with your entire life story.** Stories are great, but these meetings are about your client, not about you. People have a natural tendency to talk about themselves. This is why you have to consciously keep yourself in check while letting your client indulge.

19. **Always accept food or drink with the utmost appreciation when a client offers it.** Again, making personal connections amplifies the rapport process. When someone can provide you with a drink, food, or other hospitality, a natural bond begins to form between both parties. Also, food and drink can lighten the mood and give you more time in front of your client for rapport building, needs analysis, and sales.

20. **Always be honest with your clients.** If you're a good liar, it will catch up to you, and if you're a bad one, it won't work. This book is all about building and improving your sales career. There will be no career for you if you lie and have to be dishonest to make sales. I've seen people do it before, and I've even seen them make a lot of money up front. Not once did they get away with it or have any kind of longevity in their position.

21. **Don't use overdone sales phrases.** For example, "Should I write that appointment down in pen or pencil?" If you're new to sales, someone will tell you within a week what a genius statement that is. People—especially business owners—have seen it all. They're solicited all of the time, and their defenses go flying up when they hear things that make you sound like just another salesperson. Talk like a normal human being if that's how you want to be treated.

22. **Don't refer to yourself as a consultant.** Every sales-person tries to soften the sales process by pretending he is a consultant in his industry. It's a canned statement, and if the client ever looks to you as a consultant, it won't be because you told him that you're one. It's an earned trust. Over the years, you may develop into a consultant for your industry. However, you cannot be a legitimate consultant if you're always implying that your product or service is the end-all, be-all for all needs related to your line of business.

23. **Never get in a fight with your client.** It's possible to have disagreements, but puffing up your chest and trying to put your client in her place is just plain stupid. Customers can be frustrating. Keep your calm and deal with them construc-tively. If things get too heated or out of hand, walk away from the business or ask your manager to get involved.

24. **Be kind to the people in your client's business, party, or family.** If you're a jerk to any of them, it'll get back to your client. I once had a client who would call his receptionist back into the office a few minutes after a sales rep showed up. He would ask her how she was treated and what she thought of the person waiting out in the lobby. Not every-one will go to that extreme, but there will always be conver-sations between clients and their associates. There's nothing wrong with being the salesperson everyone likes!

25. **Even if you have an answer ready to go the second a client asks you something, consider taking some time to prevent your response from sounding canned.** In time, you will become an expert on your product and industry. A wealth of information will be at your fingertips, and you'll be temped to flaunt it every chance you get. Take your time and let it come out in a natural conversation. You can even redirect the client's questions with some questions of your own before you fire back.

    **Client:** How good is this guarantee compared to your competition's?

    **You:** As far as the length of the guarantee or how comprehensive the coverage is?

    Instead of diving into some killer speech you've spewed forth a dozen times before, turn it into a non-mechanical conversation.

26. **Don't give your client advice on anything outside your industry unless she asks you to do so.** Sometimes you will be sitting with your client, and she'll be talking to someone else to respond to a brief interruption or concern. Your stroke of genius may be in direct contradiction to what she was thinking on the subject.

    **Client:** Can you hold on one second? I have to tell my wife something. Mary, Zimmerman's Restaurant sounds like a good choice for tonight.

    **You:** Oooh, are you sure about that? I heard their food sucks!

    **Client:** Interesting. It's my brother's restaurant....

    It's an extreme example, but you see where I'm going.

27. **Laugh at your clients' jokes.** Only if you're certain it's a joke, though! Just like smiling and being agreeable, you should have a sense of humor. This doesn't mean you should tell jokes yourself, because you won't know your clients' real sensibilities for some time.

28. **Ask for confirmation throughout the entire sales process (unless you're in retail).** The continual "yes" answers prime the client for a final "yes" and allow you to handle any objections as soon as they're a concern to your client. If you don't give him an out for objections, he'll hold onto his concern until the end and not register anything else you've said from that point on. Also, if you get to the end of a conversation littered with yes answers, the client will have a hard time qualifying a big, fat "no."

29. **Don't make excuses when you come up short.** If a sale falls through, you should have plenty of other things working that can quickly fill the void. There may be some extenuating circumstances that killed the sale, but it's entirely your fault for not having more business to take its place. If you don't take personal responsibility for your shortcomings and failures, you will never grow or learn. Taking on responsibility also allows you the chance to right your wrongs. When you pass things off to excuses, they're gone, and there's nothing left you can do to improve your circumstances.

30. **Don't judge a book by its cover.** You never know. You might think someone surely can't afford something or wouldn't be a good candidate for your product or service, based on your bad first impression, but you never know until you do a needs analysis. It doesn't matter what someone looks like or how her home or office looks; different people operate in different ways.

31. **You cannot sell on budget.** Your managers will tell you to get a budget as early as you can so that you don't waste your time. When you sell based on needs, budget is only an objection. If the customer simply cannot afford what you've proposed, you can make changes. If someone needs a dump truck but he can only afford a wheelbarrow, he's not going to be able to do what he set out to do.

32. **Follow up on all sales.** No matter what your industry is, follow up on every sale you can. Some businesses don't collect enough information to do so, but any that do should take full advantage. You might feel as if your sale is very transactional. Someone buys a product or service from you, and maybe you'll never see her again. The value of following up is limitless. You will be going an extra step for customer service, and you'll get repeat and referral business.

33. **Cold call and prospect.** The key to success in sales is prospecting. I've made it clear throughout this entire book, and I will close with one last reminder: No matter what happens throughout your entire sales process, prospecting is the most crucial step.

# Index

## S

# Like the Book?

**Let us know on Facebook or Twitter!**

facebook.com/courseptr

twitter.com/courseptr

Fan us on Facebook or Follow us on Twitter to learn
about upcoming books, promotions, contests, events and more!